# How a Business Works

What Every Businessperson, Citizen,
Consumer, and Employee Needs to Know
About Business

by

William C. Haeberle

authorHOUSE®

*AuthorHouse™*
*1663 Liberty Drive, Suite 200*
*Bloomington, IN 47403*
*www.authorhouse.com*
*Phone: 1-800-839-8640*

*First published by AuthorHouse 6/19/2008*

*ISBN: 978-1-4343-9215-2 (e)*
*ISBN: 978-1-4343-9214-5 (sc)*
*ISBN: 978-1-4343-9216-9 (hc)*

*Library of Congress Control Number: 9781434392145*

*Printed in the United States of America*
*Bloomington, Indiana*

*This book is printed on acid-free paper.*

# ACKNOWLEDGMENTS

Dr. Judith Spector, Professor of English and Head of the Division of Liberal Arts at Indiana University Purdue University, Columbus, has been a mentor, a colleague, and a writing instructor for me. She graciously served as an editor for this book. She helped inspire me to write this book. Her writing instruction gave me the skill and confidence to tackle this writing project.

Dr. William L. Haeberle, Professor Emeritus of Management at Indiana University, provided wonderful input and insight as an editor of the business content for this book. His mentoring and support have helped me improve this book with every draft.

Hannah Bolte served as the editor of the final draft of this book. Her knowledge of writing and business, plus her keen eye, resulted in many improvements to the final draft.

Dr. Georgia Miller, Head of the Division of Business at Indiana University Purdue University Columbus, gave me my start at Indiana University by hiring me as an adjunct instructor. One year later, I became a full-time faculty member. She has been a mentor to me and a valuable resource for me in my various roles at the university.

Without the support of my family this book would not have been possible. I include both my immediate family and my extended family – their support and friendship are most appreciated. They have always been there for me.  I would like to express a special thank you to my sister, Patricia Haeberle; my brother, David Haeberle; my sister-in-law, Beth Haeberle; and my father, William L. Haeberle.

Finally, I would like to thank my students.  They inspired me to write this book.  While I knew what to write, they helped teach me how to write it.  It is my intention to continue learning from them. They are the reason why I love teaching and always look forward to the next class.

*I dedicate this book to my mother, Dr. Yvonne C. Haeberle. She would have enjoyed my writing and publishing this book.*

# TABLE OF CONTENTS

# PREFACE

My goal for you in reading <u>How a Business Works</u> is not to understand everything about business after you have finished reading the book. To accomplish that, the book would need to be very, very long. The goal is to create a *framework* for understanding business in 12 chapters that you can read, understand, and apply in a relatively short period of time. This framework will serve you in three ways:

1. It will help you to understand the behavior of sellers and employers, so that you can be a more informed businessperson, citizen, consumer, and employee.
2. It will help you to predict the future behavior of sellers and employers, so that you can make better plans and achieve better outcomes as a businessperson, citizen, consumer, and employee.
3. It will give you a basic understanding of business (a framework), so that you can effectively and efficiently learn more about business and organizations from the perspectives of your roles: as a citizen, consumer, employee, and possibly businessperson.

Some examples of the kinds of questions we would like to be able to answer as a result of reading this book and developing a framework for understanding business are:

- As a businessperson:
  - How do my decisions and actions affect the revenue and expenses of my organization?
  - How can I increase revenue and decrease expenses in my organization?
  - How can I operate ahead of the curve (know what is coming and be prepared for it)?
  - How can I best serve my customers?
  - How can I add more value to what I do in the marketplace?
  - Should I love, or dislike my competitors?

- As a citizen:
  - What are the characteristics of a good employer for my community, my state, my country, and the world?
  - Is globalization a good thing for me, my community, and my country?
  - How can I get globalization to help me, rather than hurt me?
  - How do the purchasing decisions that I make affect my community, my country, and the world?
  - What should the role of government be in business and economic activity? Is there a relationship between government regulation and the prices paid by consumers?

- As a consumer:
  - How can I choose the best sellers for the goods and services that I purchase?
  - How can I determine what is the best price for the goods and services that I purchase?
  - How can I ensure that I will get what I think I am getting when I purchase goods and services?
  - How can I spot consumer opportunities in the marketplace?
  - How can I avoid unpleasant buying experiences?
  - How can I get the most for the money that I have to spend?
  - How can a seller's brand help me in my purchasing decisions?

- o As an employee:
  - o How can I determine if a company or organization will be a good place for me to work – both now and in the future?
  - o Is my company or organization a good place to work?
  - o Will my company or organization be a good place to work in three months? One year from now? Five years from now?
  - o Will my company or organization be a good place to receive promotions, pay raises, or bonuses in the future?
  - o How can I make myself more valuable to my employer? Which of my activities are helping my employer, and which of my activities are hurting my employer?
  - o How can I better serve my company's customers?
  - o How can I spot good employment opportunities?
  - o How can my company benefit from globalization, rather than be hurt by it?
  - o How can I get advancing technology to help me?
  - o How can I deal with all of the information that is out there?

In addition to providing a framework for understanding business, this book can be used as a handy refresher…you can do a quick review of any of the 12 chapters whenever you need to do so – quickly and efficiently.

As you begin the book, keep in mind the questions listed in this preface. Try to begin answering these questions. And begin thinking of your own questions that you would like to answer.

I wish you success in your study of business.

William C. Haeberle

Please visit: www.howabusinessworks.com

# CHAPTER 1

## *Introduction To Business*

The framework for understanding business comes in 12 parts that are divided into 12 chapters. Chapter 6 – How a Business Works, pulls together the first six chapters. Chapter 12 – Today's Business, brings together all 12 chapters. Key to understanding how a business works is a clear understanding of Chapter 6. I would encourage you to study Chapter 6 after you have finished reading the book.

Throughout the book, I will use the word *product* to describe physical goods, services, or a combination of physical goods and services. Product will simply mean that thing that a seller sells to produce sales revenue. Sales revenue is a form of income. It is the part of income that comes from selling that thing that a seller sells (the product) and generally represents the majority of a seller's income.

To start, you need to understand the following:

*THE LESS COMPETENT AND LESS
KNOWLEDGEABLE SELLERS ARE GOING
OUT OF BUSINESS EVERYDAY.*

\* *The author uses gender neutral English.*

1

*ONLY THE GOOD SELLERS ARE
PROSPERING.*

*IN THE FUTURE, ONLY THE BETTER
SELLERS WILL PROSPER.*

Today's marketplace is more competitive than ever before in history. The successful seller must be better at doing what it does than ever before in history. This provides great opportunities and benefits for:

o   Consumers receive better quality products and more choices at lower prices. If one seller does not get the job done for the consumer, the consumer can usually find a seller that can.

o   Employees that have advanced job skills can command larger wages or salaries with greater job security.

o   Business people that have advanced management skills can enjoy business more than ever before.

o   Sellers have the opportunity to differentiate themselves from competitors and be noticed by consumers by delivering superior products. Good competition can make a seller better at what it does than if it did not have any strong competitors.

OK, so what exactly is a business? Businesses are private producing units of goods and services in our society. A business will attempt to have its income exceed its expenses. The difference is called profit. If expenses exceed income, the difference is called a loss. To stay in business, a firm must, on average, have a profit. This is true for all types of organizations; schools, churches, universities, and local governments all must, over time, have income that exceeds their expenses. The same is true for individuals. For individuals, the result is savings by the individual. For business, profits are reinvested back into the business, or are distributed to the owners of the business. For not-for-profit organizations, profits are used to provide more service to those served, or to reduce prices (such as a not-for-profit hospital), or to reduce taxes for taxpayers if a governing body.

*Income − Expenses = Profit*
*or*
*If Expenses exceed Income, there is a Loss.*

To make a profit, a business must satisfy a need or needs of customers. To satisfy customer needs, the business must have offerings (physical goods and/or services) that people want.

To make a profit and satisfy need(s) a business must organize resources. There are four general categories of resources:

o **Human** - people who furnish their work in return for pay (employees)
o **Material** - physical things - like buildings, machinery, and raw materials
o **Financial** - the money required to organize and operate the business
o **Information** - tells business managers how effectively the other resources are being combined and used

To summarize, a business must do three things to be successful:

o **Organize resources**
o **Satisfy a need or needs**
o **Make a profit**

## Business Classifications

Businesses are generally classified as one of three types:

o Manufacturing (makers of physical goods)
o Services (providers of services)
o Marketing Intermediaries (Target, Kroger, Wal-Mart)

## Various Names for a Business

A business can be called several names, including: a firm; a business; a seller; an organization; and a company. In addition, the name "corporation" can be used if the business is incorporated. If the business is organized as a partnership, it could also be called a partnership. A business organized as a limited liability company could also be called an LLC or a limited liability company. We will review the various forms of business ownership in Chapter 4.

### Inside a Business

Now let's take a closer look inside a business to get a picture of what its parts are like. A business has three *functional* areas:

o **Finance** is responsible for the acquisition and allocation of capital (money) for the firm. (Chapter 9)
o **Marketing** creates and manages demand for the product of the company. Marketing sells the company's product. (Chapter 8)
o **Operations** makes the product. (Chapter 7)

In addition, a business has *support* areas:

o **Accounting** records, estimates, organizes, and summarizes financial and operational activity. (Chapter 5)
o **Human Resources** is responsible for finding the right people to work in the firm, to help keep the right people in the firm once they are there, and to forecast future people needs. (Chapter 10)
o **Information Systems** provides the appropriate technology systems and information to facilitate the operation of the business. (Chapter 11)

### Systems Thinking

To successfully operate a business, a business manager must use what is called **systems thinking**. The idea of systems thinking is that the manager must get all the parts of the business working together, and that all the parts are interdependent upon one another. No part is more important than another, as all parts of the system must be working for the business to be efficient and successful. The business is thought of as a "system." The whole is greater than the sum of its parts.

An example of a system is the human body. The parts of the body, such as the heart and brain, cannot function without the other parts of the body. How a part functions affects the other parts. The whole of the body is greater than the sum of its individual parts.

What the customer experiences does not just happen…what happens is the result of the efforts of business managers who must visualize the customer experience and then fit together the processes that are needed to create a system to get the job done. A **process** in business is any series of steps that are followed to carry out a task or activity. Systems thinking is one of the really fun parts of business management.

### The Value Chain

The value chain consists of all the major activities that add value to the firm's products. Each activity is necessary to deliver a product to the customer and generate sales revenue.

## Business Activities Making Up the Value Chain

*Research &→ Product→Operations→Marketing→Distribution→Customer*
*Development Design                                     Service*

The flow of activities is from the left to the right. Depending on where you are on the value chain, everything to your left is an "upstream" activity and everything to your right is a "downstream" activity. For example, if we are looking at the marketing activity…then operations, product design, and research & development are upstream activities, and distribution and customer service are downstream activities.

A separate company may complete each of the activities in the value chain. If a company carries out more than one activity, it is **vertically integrated**. Vertical integration is very common. Some sellers control all the activities in the value chain; from the production of raw materials, to final distribution of products to consumers and after-sale service. Other firms focus on just one part or a few parts of the value chain.

### Value-Added Activities and Non-Value-Added Activities

An activity that does not add value to the product for which customers are willing to pay is considered a non-value-added activity. Non-value-added activities increase the seller's expenses and result in a higher price, but the customer does not desire them enough to actually want to pay for them. The customer would like to pay for only those activities that add something to the product that the customer needs or wants. Thus, a focus of successful sellers is on spending resources on activities that add value to the product and eliminating activities that do not add value. This is the seller that can provide the best price and value to the customer.

**Remember that the customer decides what adds value and what does not add value...the seller responds to the customer.**

How can you tell if your activities at work or a feature on a product are adding value in the eyes of the customer? A good place to start is to ask your customers what they want or need. Companies that can see themselves through their customers' eyes...those that know how it feels to be in the shoes of the customer...those companies do well. Knowing the customer well leads to seeing that some activities are clearly non-value-adding and some activities are clearly value-adding activities. Others are harder to tell. I start by putting these hard-to- tell activities into two categories; what I call direct and indirect. Direct value-adding activities are easiest...you should be able with some accuracy to trace both revenue and expenses to these activities: if revenue exceeds expenses, then it is a value-adding activity; if expenses exceed revenue, then it is a non-value-adding activity. The indirect category is tougher: it is not possible or is extremely difficult or expensive to trace the indirect activity to both revenue and expenses. An example would be the company holiday party...does this activity add value or not? I like to relate these indirect activities to sales revenue.

*Indirect Activities / Sales Revenue = % of Sales Revenue*

The indirect activities should only exist if they improve the efficiency of the value-adding activities. If these activities, such as the company holiday party, actually add value to the customer, then the percentage of sales revenue measure should decline over time (meaning sales revenue goes up relative to the cost of the indirect activities). If this percentage should go up that spells trouble…it means that there are activities that are not improving the efficiency of the value-adding activities.

### The New Business Model

Another thing to note at this point in the book is that each customer wants something a little different from other customers. The old business model was where the seller would produce product and then attempt to sell it ("*push*") to customers. The new business model is that the customer "*pulls*" or demands the product…the seller then responds to the customer's "pull." To be able to respond effectively and efficiently to the customer's "pull," the seller primarily needs to:

o Be flexible: the ability to produce a product in a variety of options, colors, sizes, etc., without increasing the cost of the product or the time to make it.

o Have low setup costs and low setup time: setup costs are the costs associated with changing from one order to the next order, and setup time is the time required to change from one order to the next order. With electronic systems and advanced manufacturing methods, it is possible to have both setup costs and setup times very close to zero.

o Be able to produce and deliver the product quickly: this is the delivery cycle time that is discussed in the operations chapter. Delivery cycle time is the time from when the customer's order is received to when the product is shipped.

The result of flexibility, low setup cost and time, and low delivery cycle time is that the customer can receive a more customized product at the same or close to the same price as a mass produced product, and receive it quickly. Each customer can then receive something a little different.

# CHAPTER 2

## *Economics*

We need to look at some basic economics before moving on in our study of business. This may be a review for some and new to others. I have kept this step of understanding how a business works as straightforward as possible. I have included only what I believe to be the most important parts of economics from the perspectives of the roles discussed in the preface of this book. Let's get started with economics.

**Economics** is the study of how wealth is created and distributed. Wealth is anything of value, and how wealth is distributed is who gets what. How people of a nation deal with the creation and distribution of wealth determines the kind of economic system, or economy, that a country has.

Economics is divided into two areas:
- **Microeconomics** is the study of individual choice and how economic forces influence an individual's choices.
- **Macroeconomics** is the study of the economy as a whole... this includes things like business cycles, inflation, and unemployment.

### How Economies Differ

Economies differ in two basic ways. The first way is the ownership of the factors of production. The **factors of production** are the resources used to produce products and can be summarized as follows:

o **Natural Resources** are such things as crude oil, minerals, land, and water.

o **Labor** includes human resources such as workers and managers.

o **Capital** is money, facilities, equipment, inventories, and machines.

o **Entrepreneurship** is the willingness to take risks and the knowledge and skills necessary to use the other three factors efficiently. Another way to look at entrepreneurship is the ability to organize and get something done.

The second basic way economies differ is on how the fundamental economic questions are answered:

o **What** products will be produced? And how much of each?

o **How** will these products be produced?

o **For whom** will these products be produced?

o **At what price** will the products be sold?

### The Types of Economies

**Every economy must solve these coordination problems:**

1. What to produce
2. How much of it to produce
3. How to produce it
4. For whom to produce it
5. At what price

Capitalism (or a market economy) and socialism (command economies) are the two main types of economic systems the world has used in recent history to answer these questions.

## Capitalism or a Market Economy

The concept of capitalism is rooted in Adam Smith's The Wealth of Nations (1776). Capitalism is an economic system based on *private property rights* and the *market* in which, in principle, individuals decide how, what, and for whom to produce. The market forces of *supply* and *demand* are relied upon to coordinate those individual pursuits. The distribution of products is based on each individual's ability to purchase the products. The factors of production are owned by individuals and this ownership is protected by private property rights.

Economic freedom ensures the existence of competitive markets. *Competition* forces sellers to become and remain efficient. Both sellers and buyers can enter and exit a market as they choose. Thus, the term **market economy** is used to describe this type of system. In theory, the role of government is limited to providing protection of private property rights, education, public works, internal order, national defense, and similar items that the market is unable to provide. The government acts as a rule-maker and umpire for the economy to ensure a level playing field for all participants.

## Command Economy or Socialism

A command economy is the opposite of capitalism. The government owns the factors of production. There are no private property rights. The government decides what products will be produced, how much, how they will be produced, who gets available products, and what prices will be charged.

In theory, command economies are economic systems based on the idea that each individual will receive products based on need and not on ability to purchase the products. At first look, this seems like an OK idea – people receiving what they need. However, in practice, the government ends up forcing people to do things, and the average person lives a very difficult life devoid of choice and prosperity. Just look at the performance of command economies in past decades: economic performance has been poor and a good part of what has been produced by the command economy has gone into military spending...individuals have not gotten much of the economic output. The Soviet Union was not even able to sustain itself, much less provide a good life for its citizens.

It is said that a market economy is very good at making people unequally wealthy and a command economy is very good at making people equally poor. Which would you rather be: equally poor, or unequally wealthy?

## Competition

Competition is the rivalry among businesses for sales to customers. A seller must be efficient to be able to compete against other sellers for potential sales to customers. If a firm should become inefficient, its costs will become too high, forcing its price higher than the market price. Buyers will then choose more competitively-priced products. The inefficient seller is faced with a choice of becoming efficient or going out of business.

### The Types of Competition

Competition can be categorized into four types: pure or perfect; monopolistic competition; oligopoly; and monopoly.

**Pure Competition** has many buyers and many sellers of a product. No single buyer or seller is big enough or powerful enough to affect the price of that product. Through the forces of supply and demand, the market price is determined by the actions of all the buyers and sellers. In pure competition, price is the only dimension on which organizations compete. Few examples of pure competition exist today. The market for wheat or soybeans sold by farmers would be an example.

**Monopolistic competition** has many buyers and a relatively large number of sellers. The products are similar in nature and intended to satisfy the same need of buyers. Competition may take many forms. Firms will attempt to differentiate their product from their rivals. Burger King cooking its hamburgers over an open flame and McDonald's with its golden arches would be examples of attempts by Burger King and McDonald's to differentiate their products. Competitors hope to gain some limited control over the market price by differentiating their product. Advertising, type of distribution method, and services offered are other methods that firms use in an effort to have at least some control over price. The fast food industry is a good example of monopolistic competition. The products are all intended to satisfy the same need: the buyer's hunger. Each fast food seller works very hard to make their product seem different from rivals' products.

**Oligopoly** is a market situation (or an industry, such as the auto industry) in which there are few sellers. Typically, the sellers are quite large and large capital investments are necessary to enter the market. Thus, the market has limited entry. While each seller has a lot of control over price, competitors' prices can really affect sales. Over time, this results in similar products having similar prices. If one competitor lowers its price, the other competitors will usually follow with their own price reduction. Rather than compete over price, sellers attempt to compete by differentiating their products from competitors' products. The auto industry represents this type of competition. While the products are very similar, each seller does a great job of making their product seem different. The enormous investment required to start a vehicle-manufacturing company limits entry into the auto market.

**Monopoly** is a market (or industry) with only one seller. Utilities are natural monopolies that are permitted to exist for the public's best interest because the huge investments in capital and the duplication of facilities would be inefficient and wasteful. Government regulates these types of monopolies. A copyright, patent, or trademark is a legal monopoly issued by government to individuals or organizations to encourage the research and development of new ideas, concepts, and technologies. In some cases, one seller can become so large and powerful that it can control its market. Some people claim that Microsoft is an example of such a seller.

## Opportunity Costs

An opportunity cost is a benefit or benefits that are given up by choosing a particular course of action. To obtain a benefit, one must give up the benefits of the other alternatives.

Economic reasoning provides a framework for analysis by focusing decisions on the opportunity costs and how to measure them. Logic would indicate that one would choose the option with the greatest benefits.

## Comparative Advantage

Some resources (factors of production) are better suited for the production of one product than the production of other products. This means that some resources will have a **comparative advantage** in producing a certain type of product over other resources. The comparative advantage may show itself in lower product costs, better quality, a unique quality feature, faster delivery, greater flexibility, or superior innovation and marketing.

Opportunity costs tend to increase as we choose to produce more and more of one type of product. This is because to produce more of a certain product, we must shift resources to the production of the product...resources that are less suited to the production of that product. This is called the **principle of increasing marginal opportunity cost**, stated as follows:

*In order to get more of something, one must give up ever-increasing quantities of something else.*

Initially, the opportunity costs of producing a product are low because we use resources that are well suited to that product's production. As we produce more and more, we begin to use resources that are less suited to the product's production...and we use resources that are well suited to the production of other products.

If a country can produce a product at a lower opportunity cost than another country, then the country has a comparative advantage. Remember, this means that the country has a lower opportunity cost, not necessarily a lower absolute cost. An absolute advantage would be the ability to produce a product at a lower cost than any other nation.

## Supply and Demand

### Demand

People *demand* much less than they *want*, because the term "demand" means a willingness and ability to pay. So remember, in economics, "demand" and "want" are two very different things. For example, I may want a 32-inch LCD TV, but I am not demanding one. I am not willing to pay the current price for the TV. However, if the price were to lower I would demand one; in other words, I would purchase the TV. This example illustrates an important aspect of demand. Demand will change as price changes. At a very high price, few people will demand the product. As the price is lowered, more and more people will demand and purchase the product. At a low price, many people will purchase the product.

Price regulates demand. If products become scarce, the price will go up and people will demand fewer products. As products become more abundant, the price comes down and people demand more products. This price mechanism is called the **invisible hand** in economics. The invisible hand coordinates individuals' demands.

The ideas expressed above are the foundation of the **Law of Demand**:
- o Other things constant, quantity demanded increases as price decreases
- o Other things constant, quantity demanded decreases as price increases

This law is fundamental to the invisible hand's ability to coordinate the desires of individuals. As prices change, people change how much of a particular product they are willing to buy. This occurs, in part, because people will substitute a similar lower-priced product for the product with the rising price or will substitute a similar falling-price product for a product whose price has remained unchanged.

The demand curve is the graphic representation of the relationship between quantity demanded and price:

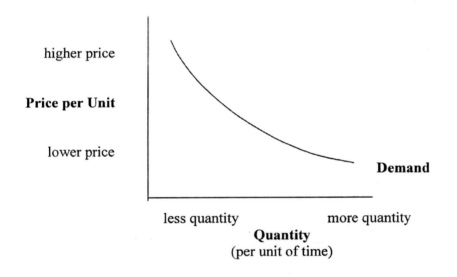

You can determine price and quantity for any number of scenarios. If you draw a horizontal line from price to the demand curve and at that point on the demand curve, draw a vertical line to quantity – the graph will tell you the quantity demanded at that price or vice versa. Try it out a few times yourself; note that as the price decreases, quantity demanded increases and as price increases, quantity demanded decreases.

### Shifts in the Demand Curve
*A change in anything that affects demand besides price causes a shift in the entire demand curve.* Shift factors include:
- o A change in people's tastes or expectations, cultural and/or social changes

o A change in people's/society's income
o A change in the prices of other products, particularly products that can serve as substitutes
o A change in taxes or subsidies to buyers
o *Anything other than price* that affects demand

A shift in the demand curve to the right would generally be a favorable shift for sellers and a shift to the left would generally be unfavorable for sellers. As an example, as DVD's became more popular with consumers, the demand curve for VHS players continued to shift to the left.


### Supply
The **Law of Supply** can be thought of as a mirror image of demand:
o Other things constant, quantity supplied increases as price increases
o Other things constant, quantity supplied decreases as price decreases

The law of supply is fundamental to the market's (the invisible hand's) ability to coordinate individuals' actions. Price regulates supply just as it regulates demand. As price increases, the opportunity cost (usually profits or growth) to firms of not supplying more product increases. Individuals and firms will rearrange their activities to produce more of the product. For example, let's assume an individual's job skills will earn that person $10 per hour in the marketplace and the person works 40 hours per week. If the price were to increase to $15 per hour, that person would probably be interested in supplying more hours of work per week. The individual would rearrange their weekly schedule to allow for more hours at work. The opportunity cost of not working increases as the wage rate increases. In the case of a business firm, increasing prices means the opportunity to earn higher profits and to grow. Managers of the company will adjust the firm's activities in an attempt to capitalize on the opportunity. This is particularly true if the firm's costs stay constant.

The supply curve is a graphical representation of the relationship between quantity supplied and price:

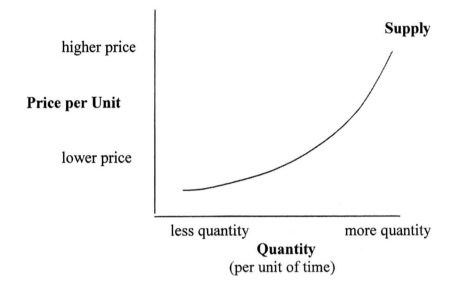

Just like demand, you can draw a horizontal line from price to the supply curve and then at that point draw a vertical line to quantity (or vice versa). The graph will tell you at that price, the market will supply that quantity of product. Note that as price increases, the quantity supplied increases and as price decreases, the quantity supplied decreases. Try it out yourself to see how it works.

### Shifts in the Supply Curve
*Shifts in the supply curve occur due to a change other than price.* Shift factors are:
- o A change in the production process because of changes in technology. Advances in technology generally increase supply.
- o The price of inputs will affect how much is supplied. If the price of inputs goes up, less will be supplied. Conversely, if the price of inputs declines, more will be supplied.
- o Supplier expectations can impact supply. If a supplier thinks

that the price will increase in the future, the supplier may choose to store its supply for sale at a later date.

o   Taxes on suppliers will reduce supply because taxes increase the firm's costs.

o   Subsidies paid to suppliers by the government will increase supply because of the decrease in the supplier's cost of production.

o   Anything other than price that affects supply

A shift to the right of the supply curve would mean that more quantity would be supplied at a given price and a shift to the left of the supply curve would mean that less quantity would be supplied at a given price.

## The Supply and Demand Curves Combined:

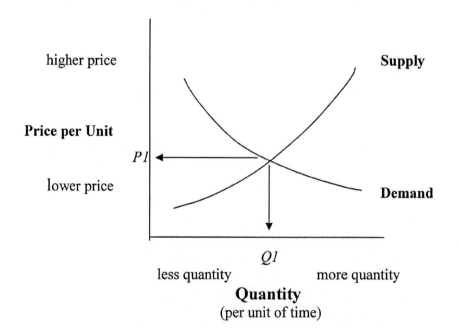

The intersection of the demand curve and the supply curve is the equilibrium point. This will be the price and quantity supplied and demanded to which the invisible hand will drive the market. The price per unit is indicated by P1 (draw a horizontal line from the intersection to P1) and the quantity is indicated by Q1 (draw a vertical line from the intersection to Q1) in the graph above.

### Excess Demand

If there is an excess of demand, the quantity demanded is greater than the quantity supplied and the price will go up. This price increase will trigger an increase in supply, a decrease in demand, or a combination of the two.

### Excess Supply

If the quantity demanded is less than the quantity supplied, the price will go down. The price decrease will cause an increase in demand, a decrease in supply, or a combination of the two.

## Marginal Costs and Marginal Benefits

Economists compare the costs and benefits of an issue and make decisions based on those costs and benefits. Economic reasoning provides a framework to approach a question. The idea is that every choice has costs and benefits…and decisions are made by comparing those costs and benefits. The **economic decision rule** is as follows:

*If the marginal benefits of doing something exceed the marginal costs, do it.*
*If the marginal costs of doing something exceed the marginal benefits, do not do it.*

A **marginal benefit** is the additional benefit received, meaning a benefit that you do not have now. A **marginal cost** is a cost that is an additional cost – over and above the costs that you have now.

## Frictions and Barriers to Global Business and Economic Activity

Next, let's look at economics from a global business and economic activity perspective. A friction or barrier to global business or economic activity is something that makes global business more difficult to do or more expensive to do. This increases the seller's costs and results in a higher price for the consumer. Here are a few examples of frictions and barriers:

- o *Fear, distrust, or dislike* by one country or society for another country or society. An example would be where one country has been invaded by another country – even many years ago... fear, distrust, or dislike can linger for many, many years.
- o *Cultural and social attitudes and beliefs* can be a restriction to global economic activity.
- o *Corruption and illegal activity* in both government and business. An example would be that in some countries, to get things done, a bribe must be paid to a government or business official.
- o An *import duty or tariff* is a tax imposed on a foreign product entering a country. There are two basic types of tariffs:
    - o *Protective tariffs* are used to protect a domestic industry from foreign competition. The idea here is to keep the price of foreign products at or above the price of domestic products. The tax adds additional cost to the foreign product, thus increasing its price.
    - o *Revenue tariffs* are used to generate revenue for the government. While the tax will raise the price of the product to consumers, its purpose is not to protect a domestic industry. The purpose of the tax is simply to increase revenue for the government.
- o To favor a domestic industry over foreign products, a country can impose a non-tax restriction that is called a *non-tariff barrier*. Some examples are:
    - o A complete halt to trading with a certain nation (or in a certain product) is called an *embargo*. Generally, embargos are used primarily as a political weapon.
    - o *Import quotas* limit how much of a product can be imported into a country during a certain time period.
    - o *Bureaucratic red tape* can be used as a non-tariff barrier. Just making things difficult or time consuming will

increase the cost of foreign products. Examples would be extremely restrictive requirements for product labeling and certification. Also, simply changing the rules frequently will add uncertainty and additional cost to foreign products.

o   Restricting the amount of a foreign currency that can be purchased or sold is known as *foreign-exchange control*. If a government limits the amount of foreign currency that importers can acquire, it effectively limits the amount of foreign goods that the importers can purchase.

o   Changing the value of a nation's currency relative to the currencies of other countries is called *currency devaluation*. By devaluing its currency, a country can make its products cost less in another country and the other country's products cost more in the devaluing country.

Try to relate the idea of frictions and barriers to your roles as a citizen, consumer, employee, and possible business person. As a consumer most people want low prices, so consumers generally want no frictions or barriers for business. A much more difficult question concerns your roles as a citizen and employee. Do you want frictions and barriers for business or not? It is confusing for business people too – you may not want any frictions and barriers in other countries, but how about here at home?

## NOW WHAT?

OK, so that is enough economics to get us started. I would encourage you to try to apply the economic concepts presented here to the next ten chapters of this book. For example, the operations function of a business is about creating supply (making the product to sell) and the marketing function is about creating and managing demand (selling the product that has been made or that can be made). How does operations know how much of the product to make? How does marketing know how much to charge for the product? We will seek to begin answering these and other questions in the remainder of this book.

# CHAPTER 3

## *Management*

I introduced business in Chapter 1 and summarized economics in Chapter 2. Next, I would like to introduce the subject of management to you.

To achieve its goals, an organization must organize the four kinds of resources. These resources are material, human, financial, and informational (as explained in Chapter 1). Management is the process of coordinating these resources. Managers must also choose the correct "mix" of resources. The "mix" will greatly influence the organization's results. In addition, the correct "mix" is always changing because of changing competition, customers, technology, culture, and governmental rules and regulations.

High-performing organizations are both efficient and effective. Effectiveness is doing the right things (such as choosing the right business goals). Efficiency is doing a good job of using the company's resources.

### The Personality Traits of Managers

Certain personality traits strongly affect how well managers can do their job. I will cover two in this book that I think are the most important traits that a manager can possess. They are an internal locus of control and emotional intelligence. Let's look at locus of control first.

### Locus of Control

People vary in their views about just how much control they have over what happens to them and what happens around them. The locus of control captures these beliefs.

A person with an **internal locus of control** believes that they are responsible for what happens to them and around them. They see their own actions and behaviors as being important determinants of important outcomes. These outcomes could be such things as promotion, work performance, and relationships with other employees or customers. These feelings help to ensure ethical behavior. The individual feels responsible and accountable for their actions.

An **external locus of control** describes someone who believes that outside forces are responsible for what happens to and around them. They do not think that their own behaviors and actions make much of a difference. They tend not to step in to solve a problem or to improve a situation.

Managers need to have an internal locus of control. Mangers need to believe that they can and do make a difference because they are responsible for what happens in an organization. If you stop and think about it, wouldn't you like all the people around you to have an internal locus of control? This would include family, co-workers, friends, etc. Employers certainly want to hire people with an internal locus of control. In my opinion, any society would be healthier if its citizens had a tendency toward an internal locus of control.

Most people are somewhere between a clear external locus of control and a clear internal locus of control. I would encourage you to make a goal to move closer and closer to a strong internal locus of control in the future. Pursuing such a goal will serve you well in your roles as a citizen, consumer, employee, and possibly as a business person.

Keep in mind that an internal locus of control is something that can be developed. This can be done in many ways, and the best way is the one that works for you. Some examples would be improving job skills through training or education or learning new life skills, hobbies, technical skills, or relationship skills. Cultivating relationships and spending time with people that have a strong internal locus of control can be of great benefit to you. Reading How a Business Works is an example of something that will assist you in developing a stronger internal locus of control. Anything that improves your understanding of why things work the way they do will help you in making more knowledgeable and thoughtful decisions...and will strengthen an internal locus of control.

My students find the idea of locus of control to be one of the most useful things that I teach. Once they get the idea of locus of control, they are able to begin incorporating it into their own lives...frequently with great success. I want you to do the same. It is a wonderful gift to give yourself and all of those around you. Keep in mind that taking blame and being responsible or accountable are two very different things. Blaming does not accomplish anything positive...either for the person blaming or the person being blamed. Blame generally does not lead to solutions or improvements. Being responsible and accountable means that you are ready to make adjustments to your behavior when necessary, to seek solutions, or to improve whatever the situation may be. Being responsible and accountable can be thought of as action oriented.

Good luck in your pursuit of a strong internal locus of control!

### Emotional Intelligence

The ability to understand and manage one's own emotions and moods and the emotions and moods of other people is called emotional intelligence. Emotional intelligence is an important aspect of effective management. A manager with a high level of emotional intelligence is better able to understand their own feelings, such as stress or doubt, and therefore will not let these feelings interfere with needed managerial decisions and actions. In addition, understanding other people's moods and emotions is an important factor in successful management. These other people could be other managers, employees, suppliers, and customers. For example, irate customers, unreasonable customers, upset employees, distracted employees, and ineffective fellow managers all require considerable emotional intelligence on the part of a manager.

Just like an internal locus of control, emotional intelligence is something that can be developed. The goal should be continuous improvement. I think that the key thing in developing more emotional intelligence is the recognition of its great importance, which then creates the desire to have more emotional intelligence. In addition, we would all like to have those around us be more emotionally intelligent.

### The Functions That Managers Perform

OK, so what is it that managers actually do? When thinking about the functions that managers perform, we can place these functions into four basic categories.

- o **Planning**: Managers must set organizational goals and decide how to accomplish these goals. We will look at goal setting in Chapter 6.
- o **Organizing**: Managers group activities and resources in an efficient and effective manner to accomplish the stated goals.
- o **Motivating and Leading Others**:
  - Motivating others is the process of providing reasons for people to work in the best interests of the organization or themselves.
  - Leading others is about influencing people to work toward a goal. Leaders strive for voluntary cooperation.
- o **Controlling**: Managers must evaluate and regulate ongoing organizational activity to ensure that the stated goals are realized. The control function is based on three actions:
  - Set standards: Standards must be set in order to have something against which to gauge performance.

Without standards, it would be impossible to know if the organization was on course to achieving its goals or not.

- Measure actual performance and compare it with the standards.
- Corrective action must be taken if there is a deviation of performance from the standards set. The purpose of corrective action is to get the organization back on track to achieving its goals and to ensure that the deviation does not happen again.

## Organizations Pay for Performance

Organizations pay managers for performance. Getting the job done is the primary determinate of managerial performance. To get the job done, managers must be able to correctly distinguish between symptoms and problems so that an appropriate solution is chosen. If a manager thinks that a symptom is actually the problem, then the manager will create a solution that will not address the actual problem and performance goals will not be attained.

It is important to remember that a problem can be either negative or positive. A problem is simply a discrepancy between an actual condition and a desired condition. An example in a business situation would be demand for a product exceeding the production quantity of the product. Most companies would consider this a positive problem. The desired condition in this example is for production to be able to satisfy demand. Businesses do not like to not have product available for sale because a potential customer may be forced to purchase from a competitor, and then may stay with the competitor's product. On the flip side, businesses do not want to have unsold products, as this increases inventory and its associated carrying costs.

Let's look at another example: a business situation where sales are declining. Declining sales is not really a problem. Instead it is a symptom of a problem or problems.

| SYMPTOM | PROBLEM | SOLUTION |
|---|---|---|
| Declining Sales | *Possible Problems*: | *Possible Solutions* |
| | -Increased competition | -New products |
| | -Not enough advertising | -More advertising |
| | -Quality change | -A quality system |
| | -Shift in demand | -New products |
| | -Distribution change | -Adjust distribution |
| | -Price increase | -Reevaluate price |
| | -Product change | -Reevaluate change |
| | -and so on … | |

Each of the listed problems for the symptom of declining sales will likely have a different solution. Of course, there are many other possible problems causing the symptom of declining sales. If the manager chooses the wrong problem then the solution developed to solve the problem will not work. For example, say the manager thinks that declining sales are caused by insufficient advertising. The solution would be to increase advertising. If, however, the actual problem is a quality change, then increased advertising probably will not improve sales.

Deciding what is the symptom and choosing the actual problem or problems (it could be more than one problem) can be tricky. And, we have not even gotten to the solution part yet. Even if the manager determines the problem or problems correctly, a workable solution or solutions must be created.

It is working with these kinds of challenges that make management a fun and rewarding profession (and high paying).

### Key Management Skills

What kinds of skills does someone need to have to do this kind of work? The key skills for managers can be summarized as follows:

- o **Conceptual Skills** are the ability to think in abstract terms. This allows the manager to see the big "picture" and to understand the relationships between the various parts of the organization. This would also include the ability to critically analyze ideas, concepts, and plans of action.
- o **Technical Skills** are specific skills to accomplish a specialized activity.
- o **Interpersonal Skills** refers to the ability to deal effectively with other people both inside and outside the company. This would include effective speaking and listening skills, writing skills, and computer skills.

### The Kinds of Managers

Managers can be classified by either their area of management, such as marketing, finance, or information systems, or by the level of management. There are usually three levels of management in large firms. In smaller, owner managed firms, the owner-manager may serve as all three levels of management.

The levels of management are as follows:

- o **Top Managers** work on the strategy of the firm and establish the goals and objectives of the organization, as well as allocating the resources to achieve them. These strategic plans are generally long-term in nature and take considerable skill and experience to create. Job titles for top managers can be president, CEO (chief executive officer), executive vice president, CFO (chief financial officer), vice president, etc.
- o **Middle Managers** develop one to three year tactical plans to implement the strategic plan, and operational plans to implement the tactical plans, which are one year or less. Middle managers coordinate and supervise the activities of the first-line managers. Job titles might be division manager, department head, plant manager, operations manager, etc.
- o **First-Line Managers** coordinate and supervise the activities of the operating employees. First-line managers spend most of their time motivating and working with their employees

and solving day-to-day problems. Job titles may be officer manager, supervisor, shift supervisor, branch manager, etc. First-line managers execute the operational plans made by the middle managers.

## Business Structure

Two or more people working together to achieve a common set of goals is a common definition of an **organization**. A **business** is a private, for-profit organization. The traditional organizational structure of a business is to organize by business function. In recent years, new types of organizational structures are appearing, such as organizing around value-creating processes.

**Line authority** is the line of authority that extends from the highest level to the lowest level of the business. This is called the **chain of command**. People with line authority are the ones that make the decisions or give the orders to achieve the goals of the business.

In contrast, a person in a **staff** or advisory position provides support, advice, and expertise to those in the chain of command. This is called advisory authority. Examples of areas of a business that provide staff and advisory support are human resources and information systems.

## Span of Management

Span of management (also called the span of control) is an important management concept. It reflects the number of people that report directly to one manager. Areas where employees do similar tasks on a regular basis can have a span of management of up to 20 employees per manager. This is called a **wide span of management** and will result in what is known as a **flat organization**. Smaller spans of five or so employees can be found where people perform varied or very difficult work. This is a **narrow span of management** and the resulting organization is called a **tall organization**.

Another way to look at span of management is by how the manager is managing; managing activities, or managing by goals. When managing activities, the span of management is lower. If managing by goals, goals are set and people determine the activities that are required to reach the goal – the manager in this situation is not concerned with the activities, but focuses on the setting and achievement of goals – the span of management is higher.

### Corporate Culture

A firm's corporate culture is defined by the heroes (frequently a founder), inner rites and rituals, and values of the business. The corporate culture can have a very strong influence on the firm's performance over time and on how its employees think and act. Public perception of the organization may also be determined by its corporate culture. Once established, corporate culture is difficult and slow to change. Therefore, a positive corporate culture is essential to long-term business success and the assessment of a culture within a business is a valuable managerial tool.

### Managing People

Frequently when people hear the word management, they think of managing people. Managing people is a part of management. Let's take a closer look at managing people.

Managing people is all about engaging people in something that you want them to do. The manager and the employee must have a meeting of the minds on what is to be accomplished (the desired outcomes).

In situations where an employee is not performing at the level desired by the manager, the following questions should be answered:
1. The first question to ask is: **Has the manager effectively communicated to the employee what is to be accomplished in the job (the outcomes and the activities to reach the outcomes)? Have the manager and employee agreed on**

**what is to be done?** This communication has as its foundation the job description. The job description needs to be clear in the employee's mind. For this to happen, the job description must first be very clear in the manager's mind. A problem with job descriptions is that the job description frequently only describes the activities of the job…the employee does not understand why they are doing the activities. An advantage of listing the job activities is that it helps everyone understand the role of the job. What is important is that besides the activities of the job, the desired outcomes of the job should also be listed and explained. Also, something that can creep into the communication process between the manager and the employee is that little by little, both the manager and the employee can change their minds about the role of the job. This slow changing of the minds can end up with a perception of not performing the job by the employee…all the while the employee thinks that they are performing the job well. The point here is this; the communication process between the manager and employee must be ongoing and documented… yes, we communicated last month, last year…but are we communicating today? Don't assume that the other person is thinking along the same lines as you are…communicate and document…then no assuming is necessary.

2. If the manager and the employee are both clear on what is to be done and there is still nonperformance of the job by the employee, it is time to ask the second question: **Does the person have the required job skills?** This is the manager's responsibility – either hire people with the skills, or provide the training so that the skills are acquired. Training only works when the employee is basically qualified for the job, but lacks certain skills necessary for the job. *It is important to remember that training only works if there is a skill problem.* Training will not solve questions #1 or #3.

3. Let's assume that questions #1 and #2 are met, but there is still nonperformance of the job. Then ask the third question: **Does**

**the employee have the needed attitude, motivation, and/or will?** It is possible to get questions #1 and #2 right and the employee can still have a poor attitude or not be motivated. If the manager mismanages #1 and #2, the employee will most likely have a poor attitude or suffer from lack of motivation. *It is important to remember that cheerleading will not help #1 or #2 – it will only help attitude, motivation, and will.* Likewise, things like bonuses and other incentives will not make up for lack of a clear job description or lack of necessary job skills.

### Summary of Managing People

A good thing to remember in the managing of people is this:

*Every problem that you have with an employee starts with you.*

Be accountable and take the responsibility…search for the causes and do not automatically blame the employee. Seek to develop a strong internal locus of control; it will serve you well in your career.

Another thing to remember is that you will not always to be able to successfully manage every person. You need to be able to realize when it just is not going to work. This is the idea of knowing when to quit…when no amount of skill or effort will make the situation work.

### The Difference between Outcomes and Activities

I have been using the terms outcomes (or goals) and activities. It is easy to sometimes confuse outcomes and activities, so let's take a closer look at the difference between the two.
- o The dictionary defines an activity as a "specified pursuit or action" and an "act of doing something." I would also like to add the concept of a process at this point in the book. A **process** is a series of activities to complete a task.
- o An outcome is defined by the dictionary as "an end result; a consequence." Another way to think about an outcome is "the

purpose toward which effort is directed." An outcome can also be thought of as a "goal" or "what I want."

The idea here is to decide what the desired outcome is, and then determine what activities and processes are required to get to the outcome. Unfocused or misdirected activities and processes will not reach the outcome. Activities and processes must be focused and directed toward the outcome. Just as some activities add value for the customer and some do not, some activities will help reach the outcome and some will not. Some activities may even hinder reaching the outcome. Obviously, it would be wise to eliminate all of the non-value adding activities and processes when working toward an outcome. Pay particular attention to eliminating those activities or processes that hinder progress toward the outcome.

## Managerial Decision Making

I want to introduce to you some of the ideas and tools that managers can use in making decisions. Forecasting, particularly the sales forecast, is one of the most important things that managers do, so I will start with it.

Forecasting is the art and science of predicting future events. *Forecasting deals with what we think will happen in the future, as compared to planning, which deals with what we expect to happen in the future.* Thus through planning, we consciously expect to alter future events, while we use forecasting only to predict future events. If the forecast is not acceptable, a plan must be developed to change the course of events to something that is acceptable.

The quality of our forecasts will make a big difference in the results of our decisions. Our forecasts will be based on assumptions that we make and the information we use. It is important to analyze our assumptions carefully to ensure that they are as accurate and realistic as possible. The gathering of reliable information is critical to good forecasting. Accurate and appropriate information will reduce *decision risk*. An inaccurate forecast leads to incorrect decisions.

There are three ways to accommodate possible forecasting errors:
1. Improve the forecasting method.
2. Improve the company's ability to change and shorten the time required to change.
3. Reduce the lead-time over which forecasts are required.

To recognize possible forecasting errors, forecasts should be thought of in two ways. First, we make our best estimate of forecast. Second, we make an analysis of the possible *deviation* or *range of error*. For example, if we are trying to forecast interest rates, the possible deviation is important. Assume that we are planning to purchase some manufacturing equipment in 12 months. We think that interest rates on equipment loans will be at 8% at the time of purchase. We also forecast that the range of interest rates on equipment loans in 12 months could be between 7.5 and 8.5%. This would indicate a stable market for equipment loan interest rates. We could proceed with our plan with some certainty and comfort. On the other hand, if we were to forecast that equipment loan interest rates could range from 7 to 11% because of unstable external factors, we would possibly adjust our plan or proceed with the original plan with less certainty. A good understanding of the possible deviation or range of error will enhance our ability to make good decisions.

*Planning* is the process of anticipating future events and conditions, and determining courses of action for achieving our objectives. The planning process creates a blueprint that specifies the means for reaching our goals. Planning defines checkpoints (sets standards) at which comparisons of actual performance with the forecast tell us whether current activities are moving us toward our objectives. Without checkpoints, we cannot define success or failure. Without standards, no comparisons of performance can be made. An example of this in business: we compare forecasted sales with actual sales results by calculating a variance.
1. *Strategic planning* is the process of determining business objectives and then adopting strategies that will eventually reach the objectives. This includes the allocation of necessary

financial, human, material, and information resources.
2. *Tactical planning* guides the implementation of activities specified in the strategic plan. Tactical plans address shorter-term actions that focus on current or near-future activities that a business must complete to implement its strategic plan.

Mistakes in strategic or tactical plans can be costly, so care must be taken in developing the plans. The strategic plan is developed first, and then the tactical plan is created.

**Types of forecasts**:
1. *Time series methods*, or trend analysis, are based on past history. The idea is that what has happened in the past will continue to occur in the future.
2. *Causal forecasting methods* attempt to develop a cause and effect relationship between variables. The idea behind causal forecasting methods is that a change in one or more variables will cause a predictable change in a variable that we wish to forecast. An advantage of this type of forecast is that it can predict turning points in a forecasted variable.
3. *Qualitative judgment methods* are forecasts based on the experience, education, and instincts of one or more individuals.

That is a brief introduction of forecasting. Next, let's look into some other ideas and tools that can be used in decision making.

**Contingency Planning** – Contingency planning takes into account the real options that are part of a decision, project, or process. The goal is to explore the dynamics of the decision or activity and to investigate the real options. The thought process is about considering some of the possible future situations and what actions we are going to take if they should occur.

**Data and Information** – While many people use the terms data and information interchangeably, the two are actually very different. Data are verbal or numerical descriptions that are usually the result of some sort of measurement. The word "data" is plural and the singular form is "datum."

Information is data presented in a form useful for a specific purpose. Thus, we must have accurate data to develop accurate information and the process of developing information from data must be in itself accurate.

**Decision Rules or Information Rules** – Decision rules can be used to quicken and simplify all types of decisions. Decision rules help to shorten the time spent analyzing choices. For example, managers attempt to simplify complex purchasing decisions, such as manufacturing equipment, by considering only a few critical factors. The factors could be such things as brand name, service and warranty, certain performance characteristics, price, etc.

Decision rules are a form of information organization and structure. It is important to remember to update decision rules as the environment or business circumstances change. I like to group decision rules into a model that I then use to manage the thing for which I have created the model. I frequently have three or four decision rules in what I call a decision model. I have found that decision models are very effective even in very complex environments. For example, a decision model that I offer my college freshmen includes three decision rules:
- o Attend class ready to work and take good notes.
- o Turn assignments in on time.
- o Ask for help when you need it.

These three things are simple and common sense, but many college freshmen struggle on one or more of these decision rules. I have observed that students who do these three things usually have a good first semester in college, and the students that don't and do things like miss class or not take good notes, miss assignments or are late on assignments, or do not ask for help when they need it – have a less successful first semester.

**The Law of Large Numbers** is a mathematical principle that states that the greater the number of something (actions, activities, products, etc.), the more likely the actual result will approximate the expected result. For example, a company making TVs will have a certain number of defective TVs returned under its warranty policy. The law of large numbers tells us that the greater the number of TVs sold, the more predictable the percentage of defective TVs will become. The seller can more accurately predict its warranty costs.

The law of large numbers highlights an important difference between consumers and sellers. For most items, such as a TV, the consumer purchases only one – the law of large numbers is not on the consumers' side – for example, a defective TV represents 100% of the consumers' buying experience. On the other hand, sellers generally sell a large number of products in a product category – thus, the law of large numbers is with them.

I look at it this way. When I am purchasing only one or a small number of a product, I know that I do not have the law of large numbers with me. I know that any problem (or lack of problems) will be 100% of my buying experience. Thus, I will take extra care in my purchase decision. I will check a reliable consumer reporting organization for its findings and the experiences of its members concerning the product I am considering purchasing. And guess what? That begins to put the law of large numbers with me – even though I am purchasing only one product. I can do this by partnering with the consumer reporting organization and its large number of members that have experienced the product.

I maintain an online subscription with such a consumer group. The cost is very low when compared to the benefits. Whenever I have questions about a product, I just log onto the consumer website and find out all about the product in question and the law of large numbers begins to shift to me. I would encourage you in your role as a consumer to use these resources.

**Opportunity Costs** – An opportunity cost is a benefit that is given up by selecting a particular course of action. For example, if a company carries large amounts of inventory and accounts receivable, one of its opportunity costs is that it has fewer financial resources to use for expansion and growth. When we decide to do something, that means that we are deciding not to do other things; these other things are our opportunity costs.

**Option to Wait** – Decisions are typically viewed as "go" or "no go." Another possibility is to wait or postpone the decision or action until another time, perhaps until conditions are more favorable. A business can be managed to provide for this "option to wait." For example, a leased delivery vehicle leaves no option to the business. At the lease expiration, the firm must turn in the vehicle and since that firm now does not have a delivery vehicle; it must acquire a vehicle to use regardless of the current conditions or financial needs of the firm. If the business owns the vehicle, it can wait to purchase the next vehicle when needed or desired. The control of the situation is more in the firm's hands.

**Pareto's Law**, or **the 80/20 Principle** states that a few items in any group constitute the significant proportion of the entire group. This concept can be applied to business situations in many ways. An example is sales forecasting where a few products usually represent the majority of a firm's sales. An accurate forecast of sales for these few products will likely result in an accurate forecast for the entire business. An important point concerning the 80/20 Principle is that not only does the imbalance exist, but that the imbalance is predictable. An awareness of the 80/20 Principle helps us to focus our attention on what is most significant. The first question is - does the 80/20 Principle apply? If it does, then what are those few items, actions, decisions, products, tasks, and so on, that are most significant?

The 80/20 Principle is another idea that my students find most useful. Many of my students begin applying the 80/20 Principle in their daily lives immediately with great success. I encourage you to try it for yourself.

An example of the 80/20 Principle in action is clothing. Most people wear 20% of their clothing, 80% of the time. The majority of a person's clothing (the 80%) is not used often (the 20%). Another example would be that most of us get 80% of our work done in 20% of the time that we are at work. A key thing to know about the 80/20 Principle is that it is not the percentages of 80% and 20% that are important; it is the imbalance that is important. The percentages could be any imbalanced relationship – 70/30, 95/5, 88/12, and so on.

We have a tendency to think that things are 50/50 or inputs = outputs. If an 80/20 relationship exists, then a relatively small input can result in a large output – this is called a 20% input or activity. Or, a relatively large input can result in a relatively small output – this is called an 80% input or activity. If you focus your attention on 20% activities, you will get a larger amount of outputs or results than if you focus your attention on 80% activities. Think about times when the result that you achieved was imbalanced to your input. You can probably think of many examples – both 20% and 80%. I find that 20% activities are more fun, rewarding, and satisfying. I think that 80% activities just seem like a lot of work.

As a final example, assume that you really love your dog. You find that spending time with your dog makes you feel good – you feel happier, you sleep better, and you feel more cheerful. If this is the case, then spending time with your dog is a 20% activity for you. The inputs (a few minutes a day) are small relative to the benefits that you receive from the time spent.

**Real Options** are the ability to delay a decision or the start of a project or process, to expand if conditions are favorable, to reduce losses if conditions become unfavorable, or to alter decisions, projects, or processes in a way that adds value.

Understanding the difference between **Relevant and Irrelevant Data and Information** is a critical managerial skill. This is the ability to distinguish between data and information that is relevant to the decision or activity and data and information that is not relevant. This can be a very difficult thing to do. Developing this skill and discipline can hardly be underestimated. Even when we know that something is irrelevant, it is sometimes hard to ignore it.

**Scenario Analysis** frequently considers the Best Case, the Probable Case, and the Worst Case scenario. When making a decision, it is helpful to consider the most probable outcome, the best outcome that can be reasonably expected, and the worst outcome that can be reasonably expected. Scenario analysis can be associated with the idea of deviation or range of error.

Assume that we are analyzing a $1,000 investment for one year. We forecast that at the end of one year, the probable case would be receiving $1,075, the best case $1,100, and the worst case $200. Is this a good investment? Based on the information given, we probably would not make this investment. The probable case is not great, the best case is not much better than the probable case, and the worst case is terrible.

Many different scenarios can be considered. The best case, probable case, and worst case are just a start.

The goal of **Sensitivity Analysis** is to find the variables that are most sensitive to change in a scenario or business situation. Changes in sensitive variables will impact the firm much more than will changes in less sensitive variables. For example, if a large percentage of a firm's expenses are in the purchase of raw materials, the price of raw materials will be a sensitive variable for the firm. The company should pay close attention to the price of raw materials.

**Side Effects** can result from decisions. Side effects can be positive or negative. For example, a positive side effect of good business planning is that to plan well, business managers are forced to think about their business in great depth and detail. A clearer understanding of the business can allow managers to see opportunities (or threats) that they could not see before.

**Sunk Costs** should not be considered in making decisions. Sunk costs are costs that have already been incurred and cannot be recouped regardless of our decisions today or in the future. Humans, despite our intelligence, have great difficulty ignoring sunk costs when making decisions. Many people are not happy to hear that sunk costs are irrelevant...instead they resist the news. Managers need to be able to identify and then ignore sunk costs, because failing to recognize the existence of sunk costs can lead to poor decisions.

### Conclusion

We are now almost ready to start looking at the functional areas of a business – finance, marketing, and operations, and the support areas of a business – accounting, human resources, and information systems. But, before we do, we need to look at one last thing – Chapter 4 - The Forms of Business Ownership.

# CHAPTER 4

## *The Forms Of Business Ownership*

In Chapter 1, I discussed the various names for a business. Some of the names, like business or company, are general names that can be used for all businesses. Other names, such as LLC or corporation, are based on the company's legal form of ownership. To make sense out of the forms of business ownership, I will first start by developing the following framework.

There are three primary differences (a framework) between the forms of business ownership that are of greatest concern to most people.

1.  Unlimited and limited liability:
    o  *Unlimited liability* means that both the business assets and the business owners' personal assets can be legally pursued by creditors to pay business debts.
    o  *Limited liability,* on the other hand, means that only the business assets can be pursued by creditors to pay business debts. The business owner or owners' personal assets cannot be pursued by creditors. Thus, liability is "limited" to business assets. The legal concept of limited liability has been crucial to the growth of the modern corporation and the subsequent economic growth.

2.  Single and double taxation:
    o  *Single taxation* is where income is taxed at just the personal level.
    o  *Double taxation* means that net income is taxed at the corporate level, and if the corporation pays dividends to the owners, the dividend income is also taxed at the personal level.

3.  Legal filing requirements:
    o  Proprietorships and partnerships have no legal filing requirements to start and stay in business.
    o  Corporations, S-corporations, and limited liability companies have legal filing requirements with the Secretary of State of the state in which they choose to file. In addition, they must also file regular status reports with their Secretary of State.

The following is a summary of the primary forms of business ownership. Try to consider the framework just discussed as you read about each form of ownership.

**Sole Proprietorship**:
o  This is the simplest form of ownership and the easiest to start.
o  There are no legal formation requirements.
o  The owner decides to be in business and begins operations.
o  The owner has *unlimited liability* for the debts of the business.
o  Net income is taxed only at the personal level, and not at the business level.

**Partnership**:
o  *Two or more persons* act as co-owners of a business.
o  A written formation agreement is not required, but is recommended.
o  It can or it combines the skills and resources of more than one person to create a competitive advantage in the marketplace.
o  Each general partner has *unlimited liability* for the debts of the business.

o Net income is taxed only at the personal level, and not at the business level.

## Corporation:

o It is an *artificial person* created by law, with most of the legal rights of a real person.
o There is ownership of stock, and stock is easily transferred from owner to owner.
o *Stockholders* (owners) elect a *Board of Directors.*
o The Board of Directors represents the Stockholders.
o The Board of Directors appoints the *Corporate Officers.*
o *Public (Open) Corporation*: A corporation's stock is bought and sold on security exchanges and can be purchased by anyone. Public corporations must disclose their operations and activities to the public.
o *Private (Closed) Corporation*: The stock is not sold to the general public; it is usually owned by a relatively small number of people. Public disclosure of activities is not required.
o A business is allowed to incorporate in any state that it chooses.
o *Limited liability*: The owners are not responsible for the debts of the corporation; the owners have only their investment in the company's stock at risk.
o The corporation has *perpetual life*. Since the corporation is a "legal" person, it exists independently from its owners, and therefore survives them.
o Taxed on its net taxable income, a corporation can divide its net after-tax income in two ways. The company can retain its after-tax income to use in the business; this is called *retained earnings*. Or, the firm can distribute all or a portion of its net income after tax to the stockholders; these are called *dividends*.
o Dividends will be taxed as income for the stockholder resulting in *double taxation* (taxed at the corporate level and taxed again at the stockholder level).

## S-Corporation:

o It is an *Internal Revenue Service designation.*

o If certain requirements are met, the directors can apply for S-Corporation status, which means that the corporation is taxed as if it were a partnership (avoids double taxation).

o It retains *limited liability.*

o Some of the IRS requirements are: no more than seventy-five stockholders are allowed; stockholders must be individuals, estates, or certain trusts; and there can be only one class of stock. In addition, all stockholders must agree to elect to become an S-Corporation.

### Limited Liability Company (LLC):

o It provides *limited liability* to owners.

o It is taxed like a partnership (avoids double taxation).

o It is approved in all 50 states.

o It combines the benefits of a partnership and a corporation.

o There are fewer restrictions on the number of owners and on who can be an owner.

o Owners are called *members.*

### Resources

There are many good sources of free information concerning the forms of business ownership, starting and operating a business, and the taxation of business. The following are a few of the main governmental resources:

o Contact the Indiana Secretary of State for information and forms for the formation of the various entities that we have discussed: www.in.gov/sos/, or the Secretary of State of the state in which you are interested.

o For information and federal taxation forms, go to: www.irs.gov/.

o To obtain a Federal Employer Identification Number, which is also called a Federal Tax Identification Number go to www.irs.gov/.

o For information on starting and operating a business: www.irs.gov/ and www.in.gov/sos/, or the office of the Secretary of State of the state in which you are interested.

o   For information relating to taxation for the State of Indiana: www.in.gov/dor/business. Each state should have a similar information website.

## Exhibit 4-1

Here is a summary of the forms of business ownership. I have included a bit more taxation information and included some of the IRS form numbers and schedules for those thinking about starting their own businesses. For future business owners: while all of this may seem like a lot, keep in mind that you only need to know about one form of ownership – the one that you choose.

| | Proprietorship | Partnership | Corporation | S-Corporation | LLC |
|---|---|---|---|---|---|
| **_Liability_** | unlimited | unlimited | limited | limited | limited |
| **_Documentation_** _or_ **_Formation Process_** | none | Partnership Agreement between Partners | Articles of Incorporation | Articles of Incorporation | Articles of Organization |
| **_Income Taxation_** | | | | | |
| Business Return: | none | Partnership Return Form 1065 | Corporate Return Form 1120 | Corporate Return Form 1120S | none |
| | **No tax paid** | **No tax paid** | **Tax paid** | **No tax paid** | **No tax paid** |
| Information Form | | K-1 | Dividends | K-1 | |
| Personal Return: | Schedule C Form 1040 **Tax paid** | Schedule E Form 1040 **Tax paid** | Schedule B Form 1040 **Tax paid on dividends** | Schedule E Form 1040 **Tax paid** | Schedule C Form 1040 **Tax paid** |

# CHAPTER 5

## *Accounting*

The purpose of the accounting chapter is to begin to be able to read and understand accounting information – the basic set of financial statements. Just about everybody at various points in life needs to be able to understand financial statements...at a school board meeting, making a mortgage application for the purchase of a new home, making decisions for the investment of your retirement funds at work, determining if an employer offers you a good place to work, deciding on how to fund a child's college education, determining which sellers from which to purchase products...to name a few examples. Let's get started with learning about what accounting does and some of the uses in business for the basic financial statements.

Accounting is the process of recording, estimating, organizing, and summarizing financial and operational activity. Financial information is primarily reported on three financial statements:
- Balance Sheet
- Income Statement
- Statement of Cash Flows

The statements are summaries of financial transactions and are pretty much the same regardless of the size and type of business. The primary users of accounting information are the managers of the firm.

Accounting information is first and foremost management information. Managers use the information to plan and set goals, organize resources and activities, lead and motivate employees, and control the business.

Other users of accounting information are:
o   Government agencies – to calculate taxes the firm must pay various governmental units (federal, state, local), and to approve new issues of bonds and stocks by the firm (Securities and Exchange Commission for federal; in addition, each state has its own securities agency).
o   Potential investors and current stockholders – to judge the financial health and future prospects of the firm for the purpose of purchasing or continuing to own the firm's stocks or bonds.
o   Lenders and suppliers – to evaluate the credit risk of the firm before lending money or extending credit to the firm.
o   Employees and potential employees – to help determine if the firm will be a good employer both today and in the future.

When looking at financial statements, you will see some numbers that look like this:  $(7,500)…in accounting that means minus, or a negative number…in this example minus 7,500 or a negative $7,500. If a number has a <u>double underline</u>, that means that the number is a total.

### The Difference between Financial and Managerial Accounting
The purpose of **financial accounting** is to create reports, generally by using the financial statements listed at the beginning of this chapter, for those outside the organization:  government agencies; potential and current stockholders; lenders and suppliers; and employees and potential employees.  The emphasis is on summarizing the financial consequences of past activities using the financial statements.  These reports are mandatory and must follow *generally accepted accounting principles (GAAP)*.  Precision is required, but only summarized information for the entire company is presented.  The cost of creating the reports is not considered, since they are required.

**Managerial accounting** creates reports for those inside the organization for managerial purposes. The emphasis is on helping make decisions that affect the future. Generally accepted accounting principles (GAAP) do not need to be followed. The relevance of information and receiving it at the appropriate time are emphasized. Detailed reports relating to a wide variety of activities in the organization, such as a product, a product line, a customer, an individual machine in a factory, a factory, a department, a business segment, etc., are prepared. Managerial accounting is not required, so the cost of creating the information is compared to its benefits. If you were to ask someone working in managerial accounting in which part of the company they worked, they would probably say finance.

### The Accounting Equation

The accounting equation shows the relationship between assets, liabilities, and owners' equity:

$$\text{Assets} = \text{Liabilities} + \text{Owners' Equity}$$

**Assets** are the resources that a firm owns. **Liabilities** are the firm's debts. And owners' equity is the difference between assets and liabilities. **Owners' equity** is the amount that would be left over if all the firm's assets were sold and all debt was paid off.

### The Balance Sheet

The balance sheet is a summary of the firm's assets, liabilities, and owners' equity. A balance sheet represents a moment in time or snapshot of the firm's financial position. Every time a business has a financial transaction, the balance sheet changes.

A balance sheet can be summarized like this:

> **Current Assets**
> *plus* **Fixed Assets**
> *plus* **Intangible Assets**
> **Total Assets**
>
> **Current Liabilities**
> *plus* **Long-term Liabilities**
> **Total Liabilities**
> *plus* **Total Owners' Equity**
> **Total Liabilities + Owner' Equity**

The accounting equation must apply:

## Total Assets = Total Liabilities + Total Owners' Equity

### Assets

Assets are listed from most liquid to least liquid. *Liquidity* is the ease with which an asset can be converted into cash. A liquid asset is one that can be converted into cash easily, quickly, and without loss of value.

**Current assets** are liquid assets or assets that will be used, sold, or collected in one year or less. Generally, three categories of current assets are used on balance sheets: cash, accounts receivable, and inventory. *Cash* is cash on hand, checking accounts, savings accounts, short-term investments, etc. *Accounts receivable* are amounts owed by customers to the business. Accounts receivables result when a firm sells on credit to customers. Customers are then required to pay the business within a specified time period, usually 30 to 60 days. *Notes receivable* are receivables for which customers have signed promissory notes due within a year or less for the amount due the firm. *Inventory* is the value of products that a business has on hand for sale to customers. *Prepaid expenses* include items such as prepaid insurance, office supplies, and prepaid rent. Prepaid expenses are usually listed last because they will be used rather than converted to cash.

**Fixed assets** are assets that are used or held for longer than one year. Fixed assets are things like buildings, equipment, machinery, and land. Fixed assets are generally not for sale, but instead are used to produce the products that the firm sells, or to facilitate sales (such as a delivery truck). Most fixed assets lose some of their value each year. This reduction in value is called *depreciation*. Accounting systematically keeps track of depreciation by first estimating the useful life of a fixed asset when it is first purchased, and then reducing a portion of the cost of the fixed asset each year based on its useful life.

**Intangible assets** are assets that have a value, but do not exist physically. Intangible assets usually give a business certain privileges or rights. Examples are patents, trademarks, franchises, goodwill, and copyrights. A patent is an exclusive right granted to its owner by the federal government to manufacture and sell a patented item, or to use a process for 17 years. A trademark or trade (branded) name is a symbol, phrase, or name that is identified with a service, product, or company. A franchise (or license) is a set of rights that a government or a company grants to an entity to deliver a product under specified conditions. Goodwill is the amount by which a company's value exceeds the value of its individual assets and liabilities. Goodwill is not recorded on a company's financial statements unless the entire company or a business segment is purchased. A copyright gives its owner the exclusive right to publish and sell a literary, musical, or artistic work during the life of the creator plus 70 years.

### Liabilities and Owner's Equity

**Current liabilities** are debts that are to be paid in one year or less. *Accounts payable* are short-term liabilities that result from purchasing on credit such things as inventory and supplies. One firm's accounts payable are another firm's accounts receivable. *Notes payable* are liabilities that have been secured by promissory notes. Only notes payable that must be paid within one year are listed as a current liability.

**Long-term liabilities** are debts that do not require repayment in one year or less.

**Owners' equity** includes the amounts invested in the business and *retained earnings* (profits of the business that have not been distributed to owners).

## The Income Statements

An income statement is a summary of a firm's income and expenses during an accounting period. An accounting period can be any length of time, but is usually monthly, quarterly, or yearly. The length of the accounting period is typically dictated by the needs of the users of the accounting information.

If income (revenue) exceeds expenses, the firm has a profit, and if expenses exceed income, the firm has a loss.

Income statements generally come in one of two formats: the **traditional approach** (also called the functional format), where expenses are organized by function using a concept called *absorption costing*, and the **contribution approach**, which organizes expenses by behavior.

### The Traditional Approach Income Statement

In the United States, tax law under the Tax Reform Act of 1986 requires a form of absorption costing to be used when filling out income tax forms. Practically speaking, for external financial reports (reports outside the organization) in the United States, absorption costing is also required. Absorption costing is the norm for external financial reports in most countries around the world.

The traditional approach income statement can be summarized like this:

**Sales Revenue**
*less* **Cost of Goods Sold**
**Gross Margin or Gross Profit**
*less* **Operating Expenses**
**Net Operating Income**
**Other Income and Expenses**
 **Net Income before Income Taxes**
*less* **Income Taxes**
**Net Income after Income Taxes**

*Sales revenue* is the dollar amount that a business receives from selling products. *Cost of goods sold* is the cost of producing or providing those products. *Gross margin (also called gross profit)* is the difference between sales revenue and cost of goods sold. *Operating expenses* are all business operating costs other than cost of goods sold. Frequently, operating expenses will be divided into two categories: selling (or marketing) expenses and administrative expenses. *Selling expenses* are the costs of selling the product and *administrative expenses* are the firm's organization-sustaining expenses (the costs incurred in managing the business), such as administrative salaries and wages, main office space and expenses, and expenses associated with filing income tax forms and other government reports. *Net operating income* is how much money was made from the operations (doing that thing that the business does) of the business. Net operating income is an important number because it tells you if that thing that the business does is worth doing.

*Other income and expenses* are those incomes and expenses that are not part of the operations of the firm. Examples are: interest expense or interest income; sale of a fixed asset; and gain or loss on the sale of short-term investments, such as U.S. government securities. *Income taxes* are the income taxes paid by the firm to the various taxing authorities. *Net income after income taxes* is what the firm has actually earned for its efforts: *Revenue less all expenses = Net income after taxes.* This is the number that tells you if the business in total is worth doing.

When people are starting to learn about business, they frequently have trouble distinguishing between operating incomes and expenses, and non-operating incomes and expenses. Just ask yourself this question: "Does this income or expense have something to do with that thing that the business does?" If it does, then it is an operating income or expense. Let's do some examples to clarify this concept:

- A restaurant is in business to make and sell meals and service to customers. Operating incomes are sales of meals and service to customers. Operating expenses are food purchases, server wages, rent on the building, utilities, etc. – anything that has something to do with making and selling meals and service to customers. Non-operating incomes for a restaurant would be incomes that are not related to selling meals and service to customers. An example is interest earned on an account at the bank…the restaurant is not in business to earn interest on deposits at the bank…this interest income is just a side effect of being in business. An example of a non-operating expense is interest expense. Interest expense is based primarily on the amount of debt that the restaurant has…the proportion of debt and equity in the restaurant is a financing decision. A restaurant could be financed in many different ways, and how it is financed does not affect that it is in business to make and sell meals and service to customers.

- A bank is in business to take in deposits from customers, lend money to customers, and provide financial services to customers. Operating income for a bank are interest earned on loans made to customers and fees for financial services for customers (like a monthly fee for a checking account). Operating expenses would be interest paid to depositing customers, wages and salaries of bank employees, depreciation on the bank building, utilities, etc. An example of non-operating income is when a bank sells a fixed asset, such as a branch bank building it no longer needs, which produces an income. The bank is not in business to buy and sell real estate, so that income from the real estate sale (the branch bank building) is non-operating. An example of a non-operating expense for a bank is the interest expense on the mortgage on the bank building. This expense is a result of how the bank has financed its building. The building could have been financed in a number of ways, including the extremes: all equity and no debt, or all debt and no equity.

### The Contribution Approach Income Statement

The contribution approach income statement organizes expenses by the behavior of the expenses. Expenses are separated between **fixed expenses** and **variable expenses**. This type of income statement is not used for external financial reports. It is used for internal (within the organization) financial reports. The organization's managers need expenses organized by behavior to facilitate planning, decision-making, and control.

**Variable expenses** are those expenses that change proportionally with the level of business activity. Variable expenses will go up in direct proportion to an increase in business activity (usually production and sales). If business activity goes down (usually production and sales); variable expenses will go down in direct proportion to the decrease in activity.

**Fixed expenses** are the expenses that are not affected by changes in the level of business activity. Fixed expenses could change for reasons other than the level of business activity. The term fixed also suggests to people that fixed expenses are costs that cannot be controlled. This is not true. Frequently it is easier to control fixed expenses than variable expenses. Fixed expenses can sneak up on you. One tool to keep track of fixed expenses is to compute the percentage of fixed expenses relative to sales revenue. In many companies, you will see fixed expenses at about 18-20% of sales revenue. Keep in mind that the percentage of fixed expenses can vary from company to company and from industry to industry.

Fixed expenses (or fixed costs) can be classified in one of two categories: committed fixed expenses; and discretionary fixed expenses (often referred to as managed fixed costs):
  o **Committed fixed expenses (or costs)** generally relate to the investment in equipment, facilities, and the basic organizational

structure of an organization. Examples of committed fixed expenses are taxes on real estate, insurance, and depreciation of buildings and equipment. It is difficult to change a committed fixed expense once the commitment has been made. For this reason, decisions relating to committed fixed expenses should be made carefully. Committed fixed expenses possess two key characteristics. First, they are long term in nature and second, it is not possible to significantly reduce them even for short periods of time without seriously damaging the long-term goals of the organization or its profitability.

o **Discretionary fixed expenses (or costs)** are often referred to as managed fixed costs because they are just that – they are managed. They usually result from annual decisions by management to spend money in certain fixed expense areas. Examples are: advertising; internships for college students; management development and training programs; and generally, any other fixed expense that can be adjusted from year to year, or in some cases, adjusted within a year's time. Discretionary fixed expenses can be reduced or eliminated for short periods of time with little or no damage to the long-term goals of the organization.

A key thing to remember is that an organization's strategy may determine whether a fixed expense is considered committed or discretionary.

*So the thing to remember is that an expense is called variable if it is proportional to activity, and it is called fixed if it does not depend on the level of activity.*

An organization can have expenses that exhibit characteristics of both fixed and variable expenses. These expenses are called **mixed expenses (or costs)**. The relative proportion of each type of expense – variable, fixed (committed or discretionary), or mixed – in an organization is called its **cost structure**. A firm's cost structure will have a significant impact on its decisions and its overall competitiveness in the marketplace. An entity with a favorable cost structure will have an absolute competitive advantage over an organization with a less favorable cost structure.

The **relevant range** is the range of business activity within which the assumptions about fixed and variable expenses are valid. For example, we might know that our assumptions for fixed and variable expenses are valid for an operating range of 5,000 to 8,000 units of product. Activity levels less than 5,000 units or more than 8,000 units of product would require us to recalculate fixed and variable expenses for that level of activity. In the case of activity levels of over 8,000 units of product, fixed expenses would probably increase (we probably would need more production capacity – machines, buildings, etc.), and variable expenses hopefully would decrease with the increased volume. But, it is possible that they might increase.

The contribution approach income statement can be summarized as follows:

> **Sales Revenue**
> *less* **Variable Expenses:**
> **Variable Production Expenses**
> **Variable Selling Expenses**
> <u>**Variable Administrative Expenses**</u>
> **Contribution Margin**
> *less* **Fixed Expenses:**
> **Fixed Production Expenses**
> **Fixed Selling Expenses**
> <u>**Fixed Administrative Expenses**</u>
> <u>**Net Operating Income**</u>

**Contribution margin** is the amount remaining from sales revenue after variable expenses have been deducted. Contribution margin *contributes* toward covering fixed expenses and then towards profits for the accounting period. The sequence is important: contribution margin is first used to cover fixed expenses, and then whatever is left goes toward profits. If the contribution margin is less than fixed expenses, then a loss results for the period.

The **break-even point** is the level of sales where profit is zero, or *the level of sales where the contribution margin equals fixed expenses*. Sales levels above the break-even point result in profits, and sales below the break-even point result in losses.

The contribution margin as a percentage of sales is referred to as the **contribution margin ratio (CM ratio)**. The ratio is calculated by:

**CM ratio = Contribution margin ÷ Sales**

The CM ratio is a great managerial tool, because it shows how the contribution margin will be affected by changes in total sales. For example, assume that sales are $1,000 per year and variable expenses are $600 per year. The contribution margin would be $400 ($1,000 minus $600). The CM ratio would be 40% ($400 divided by $1,000). If sales were to increase by $100 per year, we would know that the firm's contribution margin would increase by $40 ($100 times the CM ratio of 40%).

The size of the CM ratio is very important. For example, a business with a high CM ratio can spend more on advertising to increase sales, because increased sales result in more contribution margin. Thus, organizations with high CM ratios, such as auto manufacturers, typically advertise more than companies with low CM ratios.

## The Statement of Cash Flows

The statement of cash flows shows how a firm's investing, financing, and operating activities have affected cash during an accounting period. When a balance sheet and income statement are presented, a statement of cash flows for the income statement period is also required. The statement of cash flows presents information on the cash receipts and the cash disbursements of an organization during the accounting period. Remember, the term cash usually means cash plus cash equivalents.

The amount of cash generated from operations is of particular importance. Over the long haul, a company must be able to produce a positive cash flow from its operating activities - the activities of producing and selling its products. These operating activities must over the long run provide the cash to pay off the firm's debts, pay dividends to shareholders, and provide for the future growth of the company.

The statement of cash flows can be summarized like this:

**Cash Flows from Operations**
**Cash Flows from Investing Activities**
**Cash Flows from Financing Activities**
**Net Increase (Decrease) In Cash**

*plus* **Cash at Beginning of Accounting Period**
**Cash at End of Accounting Period**

o *Cash flows from operations* are the cash generated by the firm's primary revenue source, the sale of products.

o *Cash flows from investing* activities would include the purchase or sale of fixed assets and short-term investments listed as current assets.

o *Cash flows from financing* activities include loans and loan repayments, cash dividends, and the sale or repurchase of the firm's own stock.

**Additional Thoughts on the Basic Financial Statements**
In general, a business will prosper or fail in the following order of causes:

1. The statement of cash flows is first, if there is insufficient cash, a business will not be able to continue operations, no matter how good the income statement and balance sheet look.

2. The income statement is next; the business must produce a positive net income over time to prosper and remain in business.

3. The balance sheet is third, but it is still very important. For long term prosperity, the business will need to have an improving balance sheet matched to the industry and marketplace.

### Accounting Exhibits and Business Cases

Exhibits 5-1, 5-2, and 5-3 show how the financial statements look in practice, but without numbers. You can use these blank forms to create your own financial statements. The business cases in the book include financial statements for the company in the case. These statements show you how the financial statements might look in practice with actual numbers.

### Financial Statements Tell a Story

Financial statements tell a rich story to those that know how to read them. Like many stories, at first they may be hard to understand, but with practice the story becomes easier to understand and very useful. The financial statements tell a story about where the business has been, what it has done, and what could happen in the future.

I have found that the more I learn about financial statements, the more fun they are for me. They tell me more in a more colorful way. I would encourage you to consider financial statements as a story that you can learn to have fun reading and interpreting.

**Exhibit 5-1**

# The Statement of Cash Flows

**Operating activities**:
   Net operating income                                                $
   Changes in current assets
   Changes in noncurrent assets that affect
      net operating income (depreciation)
   Changes in current liabilities
   Changes in noncurrent liabilities that
      affect net operating income              _____

**Net cash provided by operating activities**    $

**Investing activities**:
   Changes in noncurrent assets that are
      not included in net operating income    _____

**Net cash provided by investing activities**    $

**Financing activities**:
   Changes in the current liabilities that
      are debts to lenders rather than
      obligations to suppliers, employees,
      or the government
   Changes in noncurrent liabilities that
      are not included in net operating
      income
   Changes in capital stock accounts
   Dividends                                 _____

**Net cash provided by financing activities**    $
***plus* Cash at beginning of period**             $_____
**Cash at end of period**                         $_____

**Exhibit 5-2**

# Functional Format Income Statement

Sales Revenue                                              $
*less* Cost of Goods Sold                           (_____)

Gross Margin or Gross Profit
*less* Selling Expenses                            (_____)
*less* Administrative Expenses            (_____)

Net Operating Income
Other Income & Expenses                        _____

Net Income Before Income Taxes
*less* Income Taxes                                  (_____)

Net Income After Income Taxes              $_____

# Contribution Format Income Statement

|  |  | Per Unit |
|---|---|---|
| Sales Revenue | $ | $ |
| *less* Variable Expenses | (_____) | (_____) |
| | | |
| Contribution Margin | | $_____ |
| *less* Fixed Expenses | (_____) | |
| | | |
| Net Operating Income | $_____ | |

**Exhibit 5-3**

# The Balance Sheet

*Assets*
Current Assets                                    $
Cash and equivalents
Accounts Receivable
Inventory

                                          _____

Subtotal – **Current Assets**              $

**Fixed Assets**

**Intangible Assets**

                                          _____

**Total Assets**                                  $_____

*Liabilities & Owners' Equity*
**Current Liabilities**                       $

**Long-term Liabilities**

                                          _____

**Total Liabilities**                          $

**Owners' Equity**                                _____

**Total Liabilities & Owners' Equity**   $_____

# CHAPTER 6

## *How A Business Works*

The first five chapters of <u>How A Business Works</u> have laid the foundation for Chapter 6. This chapter is the key chapter of the book and should be studied, rather than just read.

A business is divided into two basic parts (see Exhibit 6-1):
o   The **business side** is about knowing WHAT to do to make money. You will hear the business side called the *hard side*.
o   The **people side** is about HOW to get it done. The people side is frequently called the *soft side*.

I think that the terms business side and people side are much better terms than the hard side and soft side. The hard side term developed because it is more quantifiable than the so-called soft side. The experienced businessperson sees the two sides as equal in importance and neither as "harder" or "softer."

### The Business Side

Some key questions on the business side are:
o   Is the business making money?
o   If so, how is the business making money?

o   How is the money-making likely to change in the future?

The business side starts with **the three parts of money making**:
o   Cash generation
o   Return on Assets
o   Growth

Successful business people understand each part of money-making and the relationships among the three parts so well that it becomes instinctive for them.

The final step on the business side is to consider the tradeoff between customers and the three parts of money making. From this consideration, business goals are developed. The business goals are about what to do to make money, and at the same time, satisfy/retain customers and acquire new customers.

### Cash generation

A business must generate cash to survive. Cash is required to pay suppliers, payroll, taxes, etc. Without cash, the business cannot operate. Employees will not work, suppliers will not deliver raw materials, utilities will not continue to supply electricity, water, gas, and telephone service, and so on. Cash gives the firm the ability to stay in business. Lack of cash, decreasing cash, or the consumption of cash means trouble…even if the other elements of money-making look good.

Cash generation is not the same thing as net income after taxes. In the long-term and in its simplest form, cash generation from an operating perspective is:

*Net income after taxes + Non-cash expenses = Cash generation*

*Non-cash expenses* would include expenses like depreciation and bad debts…they are expenses of the business…but the firm did not write a check; no cash was consumed during the accounting period for that expense.  An example of a cash expense would be payroll:  the company writes a check...cash is transferred from the business to the employee (usually electronically from checking account to checking account).

In the shorter-term, cash generation includes things like payment of accounts payable, receipt of accounts receivable, new debt financing, repayment of debt, new equity financing, repurchase of outstanding equity, and selling and purchasing assets. (See the statement of cash flows in Chapter 5)  In the shorter-term, cash generation can get complicated, but the simple truth always holds...the business must have cash to continue its operations.  Ask these questions:

o  Does the business generate enough cash?
o  What are the sources of cash generation?
o  How is the cash being used?

In the shorter-term, cash generation is the difference between all the cash that flows into the business and all the cash that flows out of the business in a given time period.  From an operating perspective, this involves the timing of:

o  The receipt of accounts receivables
o  The payment of accounts payables

From a non-operating perspective, items that affect cash are:

o  Borrowing or repayment of debt
o  Increasing equity, buying back equity, or paying dividends to (or withdrawals by) owners
o  Purchasing or selling assets

In large organizations, some people lose sight of cash...they are not aware of how their actions use cash or generate cash.  Smart business people are keenly aware of how their actions affect cash, and seek to figure out highly efficient ways to generate cash or reduce cash consumption.

Generating cash can help grow a business and improve its margins or asset velocity.  Invested wisely, cash improves the firm's ability to make money.  We will look at some ways that a company can use cash to improve its money-making ability in the next few pages.

### Return on Assets (ROA)

Assets are things in which the firm has invested...accounts receivables, inventory, equipment, and real estate would be some examples. A business uses these assets to produce its net income after taxes. Return on assets tells us how much money (net income after taxes) the company produced in relation to the assets used to produce that money.

A simple example: if you had $100 in a savings account at the bank and you earned $4 of interest last year...the $100 is the amount of assets that were used and the $4 is the return on those assets. ROA is usually expressed as an annual percentage. In this example: $4 divided by $100 = a 4% return on assets.

So, the first way to calculate ROA is what I call the accounting method:

*Net income after taxes ÷ Average total assets = Return on assets*

Notice that we use average total assets and not the total assets listed on the firm's balance sheet. This is because the balance sheet shows the total assets at one specific point in time...we want to know – on average – how many assets were used to produce the net income after taxes. Average total assets is easy to figure; for example, if a firm has prepared a balance sheet at the end of each month in a year...then add up all twelve months and divide by 12. This will give you an approximation of the average total assets of the company throughout the year.

So what is a good ROA? The best large public companies produce an annual after-tax return on assets of 10% or greater.

The problem with calculating ROA the way we have been doing is that while it gives us the ROA...it does not tell us how we did it. There is a second way to calculate ROA. I call it the managerial method, because it provides us with important managerial information and is a powerful tool in managing a business:

**Asset velocity  X  Margin as a %  =  Return on assets**

Margin is net income after taxes.  Asset velocity is:

**Sales revenue  ÷  Average total assets  =  Asset velocity**

Asset velocity (also called turnover) is NOT a percentage.  It is a number that tells us how many times greater sales revenue is than the average total operating assets used to produce the sales revenue.

Let's do an example.  The following information is provided for XYZ Company for the previous year of operations:

Sales revenue = $100
Net income after taxes, or margin = $5
Average total operating assets = $50

*Margin divided by Average total assets is $5 ÷ $50 = 10% ROA*

*or*

*Sales revenue divided by Average total assets is $100 ÷ $50 = 2 is the asset velocity*
*and*
*Margin divided by Sales revenue is $5 ÷ $100 = 5% margin as a %*

*therefore*

*Asset velocity times Margin % is 2 X 5% = 10% ROA*

Please note that the "%" is moved from after the "5" to after the "10."  Or, 2 times 5 = 10, and then you add the "%" after the 10. Move the "%" in this way every time that you calculate ROA using the managerial method.

The ROAs must match…if not, then you know that there is an error somewhere in your calculations. In this example, the ROA is 10% and we know that the ROA was obtained by generating a 5% margin (which is also called **return on sales**) and an asset velocity of 2. To increase the ROA…higher is better than lower…XYZ Company could increase its asset velocity or its margin, or both. People have a tendency to focus just on margin…smart business people have a duel focus on both margin and asset velocity.

A key thing to remember about return on assets:

**ROA must exceed the firm's cost of capital; if not, then management is destroying owners' equity.**

### Growth

Growth is vital to prosperity. To remain vibrant and alive, every person, every organization, and every national economy must grow. Not growing means lagging behind in a world that grows every day. If a business does not grow, competitors will ultimately overwhelm it. Growth energizes a business, provides promotion opportunities for employees, attracts new and talented people with new ideas, and creates all sorts of opportunities for the company. Growth is a chance to build something, to do something special, and to prosper.

But don't just use growth in sales revenue as a measure of success. Sales revenue growth in a business must be profitable and sustainable. Margins and asset velocity should improve with sales revenue growth, and cash generation must be able to keep pace. The business must know how and why it is growing in sales revenue. Is the business growing in a way that can continue into the future? The firm must watch cash carefully…is growth consuming, or generating cash?

Besides growth in sales revenue, there are other ways to grow. Examples would be: improvements in the quality of products; greater innovativeness of new products; improved processes; better customer quality or a better customer base; or more stability for the business.

*A key to long-term business success is the ability to find opportunities for profitable growth, even when others cannot.*

If margins and asset velocity are improving...and cash generation is growing, the firm will have some interesting choices:

o The company can take its cash and invest it in improving its products (adding a new feature, more colors, better quality, better customer service, etc.). The improved products will generate more demand...increasing market share...and cause sales revenue to grow, resulting in more cash generation.

o The company can take its cash and invest it in new products or industries that have the potential for substantial profits and growth.

o The firm can invest its cash in improving its processes (how it does what it does). Superior processes can create a long-term competitive advantage over rivals. With improved processes, efficiency will improve, resulting in lower costs...the business can then lower its prices, which will increase market share and sales revenue...and result in growth.

o The business can reduce its debt, which will reduce interest costs and business risk.

o The company can take some of its cash and pay dividends to shareholders or bonuses to employees.

o And so on...

**Customers**

A business must know its customers well and have a strong conviction that it cannot prosper without satisfying them. Many companies use scientific methods of market research, such as surveys and focus groups, to help understand customer and consumer needs. The best business people do not rely on clinical information alone; they know that they must be observing and talking to the people that use their products and services, or they may miss significant changes and opportunities in the marketplace. Direct contact with customers and consumers provides information and insight that other kinds of market research cannot.

I have used the words customers and consumers in the last paragraph. Are they the same, or is there a difference?

- o **Consumers** are the people that use the product…they consume it.
- o **Customers** are people or organizations to whom we sell… if we are a retailer, then our customer is also the consumer. In other cases our customer may not be the consumer. For example, assume that we make door latches for cars…our customers would be companies like Ford or Honda and the consumers would be you and me…the people that buy and use (consume) the vehicles that Ford and Honda make. A door latch manufacturer would need to understand its customers (Ford, Honda) and also the actual consumer (you and me), even though in this example the consumers are not the door latch manufacturer's customers. Why the need to always understand the consumer? Because consumer needs drive what vehicles Ford and Honda make, and ultimately the type of door latches that Ford and Honda will need to purchase.

There is a tradeoff between money-making and customers. **To be successful over the long-term, a seller must be able to both make money and retain loyal customers:**

- o A seller cannot continue to satisfy customers if it does not make money. Cash is required to make a high quality product, have good customer service, have the product available when and where the customer wants it, and so on…all things that are necessary to keep customers satisfied and retained.
- o A seller cannot make money for very long unless customers are satisfied…and continue to purchase the seller's offerings.

So, focusing on money-making at the expense of customers is shortsighted, and focusing on customers at the expense of money-making is also shortsighted. A delicate balance must be created and maintained…one that gets both jobs done…a balance that is sustainable over time.

All sellers must understand what the consumer is buying. It usually is much more than just the physical product. The consumer could also be buying convenience, service, or reliability. Frequently, the consumer is also buying the trustworthiness…of the seller.

When a business cannot get the prices and margins that it used to get, it must directly observe and talk to consumers to understand why. Everybody knows that customer loyalty is a good thing…sellers must earn that loyalty every time they come into contact with the customer. Customers need a reason to buy from a seller…the seller has to give them something that they need or want. The best way to find out what they need is to listen to them.

**Business Goals or Outcomes**

From the tradeoff between customers and the three parts of money making, business people develop desired business goals or outcomes. To figure out the RIGHT business goals, business leaders must do two things:

o Accurately perceive what is actually occurring and changing in the outside world.

o Cut through all the complexity of the outside world, and also of their businesses.

Business goals must be clear and specific…action items…that make money in the real world and retain customers. A good business manager does what no computer can do, they scan the external environment and they identify the significant events, trends, and patterns from all the things that are going on in the world…from this assessment come the business goals.

A business goal is the most important action that should be taken at a point in time. There should be about six goals. If there are too many goals, then the business will lose focus. If there are too few goals, the business will not be doing everything that it could or needs to be doing. Goals change as the internal and external environments change or evolve. The business goals should reduce complexity, both internal and external, to the basics of money-making and retaining customers. Creating business goals is a fabulous mental challenge…creating goals gives people confidence and makes them more decisive.

Goals must be communicated clearly and often. Then employees will have a better sense of what they should be doing…the organization will gain energy. If the correct business goals are chosen, the business will prosper.

*Sometimes people think that if they produce a good product and take care of their customers, the business will make money. This is not true. Money-making needs to be a part of the goals of the business.*

Let's look at **a framework for creating the right goals**. The first three goals should be financial goals:

1. A **sales revenue goal** could be a percentage increase or decrease over some benchmark (like last year's sales revenue). However, the best way to manage ahead of the curve is to state the sales revenue goal in dollars. *Sales revenue is about the volume of products sold (number of units sold) and the average sales price per unit.*

2. A **gross margin goal** is generally stated as a percentage of revenue. Many manufacturing businesses have a gross margin of 20 to 30% of sales revenue…this means that product costs (cost of goods sold) are 70 to 80% of sales revenue. Keep in mind that there is a wide range in gross margin percentages - varying with the company and the industry. Some businesses, like those in the cosmetic industry, may have gross margins as high as 80%. Companies with high gross margins will typically be in industries that have high marketing costs, and companies with lower gross margins will typically be in industries with lower marketing costs.

   a. *Gross margin is about the relationship between the number of units sold, the average sales price per unit, and the average production cost per unit.*

    b. An additional note: be sure to look at accounting methods when you are calculating gross margin percentages. For example, a company can increase gross margin by simply moving some product expenses (such as direct labor) to the period cost (operating expenses) section of the income statement.

3. **A net income before taxes goal** could be stated as a percentage or as a dollar amount. Net income before taxes could be related to the average assets used during the period, as could goals 1 and 2. The usual range is from 5 to 10% for most companies. Sometimes the percentage may be negative; the company is losing money. Net income before taxes is rarely above 15%. It is hard to get or keep a 10% net income before taxes because of competition... good competition keeps prices down, and therefore the net income before taxes percentage is kept down.
       a. *Net income before taxes is about the relationships between gross margin, operating (period) expenses and other income & expenses.*
       b. Using net income before taxes rather than net operating income, includes important expenses, such as interest expense (which is included in other income and expenses) in the firm's financial goal.
       c. Net income after taxes is not as good a goal because the business does not control its tax rate percentage. The tax rate is determined by congress and other governing bodies.

The next three goals generally fit into the framework like this:
4. A **goal to keep the product line fresh**. An example of this type of goal would be to have at least 20% of sales revenue from products introduced in the last three years. In business, it is important to regularly and successfully introduce new products because new products typically have the best margins, can attract new customers, can

energize the business, help retain existing customers, and help the business grow.

5. **Improving the quality of the customers or the quality of the customer base goal.**
    a. First, let's look at customer quality. Some customers are better than others; they are less trouble, easier to work with, more predictable, pay on time, are more profitable, ask for fewer special favors or have fewer rush orders, make larger orders, etc. In other words, the best customers consume fewer business resources for a given amount of sales than customers that are not as good. Well-managed businesses assess their customers using a customer assessment tool that ranks or grades each customer. A customer quality goal could be improving 15% of customers by one grade level or eliminating the worst 5% of the customers of the business.
    b. A business could have high customer quality, but suffer from a poor customer base. For example, suppose a business makes paint and all of its customers are good quality customers…but all of those customers are in the automotive industry. The business is at great risk if there is a down turn in the automotive industry. Improving the customer base in this example would mean finding customers from industries unrelated to the automotive industry.

6. **A keeping promises goal** could be focused on customers, suppliers, employees, lenders, owners, etc. Examples of keeping promises to customers include on-time delivery and quality within specifications. An example of keeping promises to suppliers is to be a good customer for the supplier (highly ranked or graded by the supplier). An example of keeping promises to employees could be safety in the plant (people want to come to work and know that they will not be injured), or helping employees expand their capacity

(so that they can earn pay increases). Keeping promises to lenders includes things like making payments on time, or being a quality customer for the lender (again, highly ranked or graded by the lender). Examples of keeping promises to owners are maintaining an acceptable return on assets or keeping business risk within acceptable levels. A business should always keep all of its promises. The keeping promises goal is the promise that is singled out as a promise in which the business particularly wants to focus. For example, assume that a business has been doing a pretty good job of keeping its promises, except for one area – it is frequently late in meeting its promised delivery dates to its customers. The keeping promises goal for this business should probably be to deliver orders to customers on time. Meaning, this area of weakness in keeping promises will be the focus.

**Here is a summary of the business goals framework:**
1. Sales revenue goal
2. Gross margin goal
3. Net income before taxes goal
4. A goal for keeping the product line fresh
5. A customer quality or quality of customer base goal
6. Keeping promises goal

*It is important that goals are specific and measurable. They need to be specific so that they are action items and measurable so that they can be assessed.*

## 12 Month Rolling Forecasts and Managing Ahead of the Curve

A key tool in meeting goals and managing ahead of the curve is to use a *12 month rolling forecast.* Forget about calendar years; that is old thinking. Instead, when a month of the 12 month forecast is completed…a new month is added. This keeps managers thinking 12 months into the future and *"managing ahead of the curve."*

A simple example of managing ahead of the curve is how you drive your car. You see a curve ahead…you adjust for the curve in advance…perhaps slowing the car, adjusting your position on the road, adjusting your hands on the steering wheel, stopping other activities like adjusting the radio, etc. By doing all of this, you can drive the curve under control…you have managed ahead of the curve. You are anticipating what is coming and preparing for it…in advance.

## The People Side

Understanding what to do to make money is one part of what we need to know in managing a business. The other part is executing the "how to get it done." The people side is about "how to get it done." It takes insight into people and the organization to make this happen. Delivering results is important because results energize an organization, build confidence, and provide the resources to move forward.

Unless you are a one-person business, you cannot personally execute everything required to accomplish your business goals. You will need the help of other people to get them done.

*A leader of the business knows what to do.*

*A leader of people knows how to get it done.*

*Good business people can do both.*

Being a leader of people is not the same thing as being a "people person." A leader of people has insight into how the organization really works and how to link peoples' decisions and actions to the right goals. This creates an edge in executing the business goals.

### Creating an Edge in Executing the Business Goals
o   Get the right people
o   Get those people in the right jobs

o   Expand each person's personal capacity
o   Synchronize everyone's efforts

Once everyone's efforts are synchronized, then people's energy must be channeled and released toward the right set of business goals (see Exhibit 6-1).

### Get the Right People

All businesses need the right people to be able to thrive and grow. A company could develop a model employee profile that describes the desired employee characteristics (See Human Resources - Chapter 10 for an example of a profile). The best companies will interview many people in their search for the right people.

### Get Those People in the Right Jobs

Once the business has the right people, then it must get those people in the right job. When a person is well matched to a job, they get better and better at it and they enjoy their work. As a person gets better at a job, capacity is expanded. If this process is repeated throughout the entire company, the capacity of the entire business increases.

A successful business manager knows that matching the person to the job begins with an understanding of what kinds of aptitudes, skills, and attitudes are needed to accomplish the business goals. Then they link the business need to the person's natural talent. They take the time and effort to discover people's natural talents and then place them where those natural talents will have the greatest impact.

How do you discover someone's natural talents? Watch for what tasks or activities come naturally to the person. They will energize the person...and possibly others that are around that person. When something energizes us, there is an indication of a natural talent...we can do that thing and not easily get bored or tired...so we do it a lot...and get very good at it.

### Expand Each Person's Personal Capacity

If peoples' natural talents are matched to the right jobs, there will be a natural tendency for the expansion of individual capacity. Then add selective training for additional capacity growth. If enough people's individual capacity is expanded, then the entire firm's capacity will expand.

Beyond natural talents, people need attention to do well in a job. A good leader of people enjoys helping others develop their abilities, focus their skills, develop new skills or perspectives, and use their positive energy. In other words, the leader of people loves to see people grow. The leader of people is a teacher and a coach. Teaching and coaching energizes this type of person.

### Synchronize Everyone's Efforts

We have all seen sports teams with very talented players that do not play as a team. And, we have seen such teams defeated by teams with less talented players that knew how to play as a team. Playing as a team is an example of synchronizing everyone's efforts. Organizations must synchronize everyone's efforts just like a sports team, and the synchronized efforts need to be directed toward the right set of business goals (see Exhibit 6-1).

### More on the People Side

Sometimes employees of a business get the idea that they are entitled to their customers' business. We see this cycle repeated in the real world on a regular basis. The result is that employees become overly focused on themselves and lose focus on money-making and customers (see Exhibit 6-2). A seller must earn its customers' business every day...there is no entitlement. By the same token, employees are not entitled to automatic percentage pay increases, bonuses, or extra benefits...employees must earn their wages or salary and benefits every day, and they must earn pay increases every day.

Another idea employees can get wrong is that the company is somehow responsible for their personal performance or lack of performance. The employee is responsible (see locus of control in Chapter 3)…the company will help…but the best employees know that they are responsible for their performance both now and in the future. These employees also know that over time, job skills and requirements change…they know that they must keep their job skills current; that they must continue to be able to add value to the organization every day. The better employee is always looking for new things to learn or for new ways that they can add value to the organization.

## Pulling It All Together

The following Exhibits 6-1, 6-2, and 6-3 summarize Chapter 6. These exhibits need to be studied. Take everything that you have learned in Chapters 1 through 6 into account as you study these exhibits.

Exhibit 6-1:  **A General Business Model**


Business Side
*Knowing what to do:*
*To make money & satisfy/retain customers*

People Side
*Knowing how to get it done:*
*Need insight into people & the*
*organization*

**3 Parts of Money-making**
  -Cash Generation
  -ROA
  -Growth

**Employees** - Getting It Done
-Get the right people
-Get those people in the right jobs
-Expand their personal capacity
-Synchronize everyone's efforts

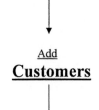

Add
**Customers**

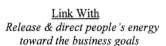

Link With
*Release & direct people's energy*
*toward the business goals*

Develop
The right **Business Goals**
  (or Outcomes, Priorities)
*Understanding how to make money:*
*Must cut through the complexity of*
*the real world & the organization*

## Exhibit 6-2

Let's take Exhibit 6-1 and isolate three significant areas: money making, customers, and employees.

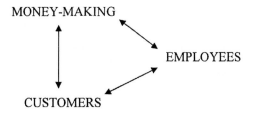

For a business to be successful over the long term, it must make money, satisfy and retain customers, and be a productive place for people to work:

- o **Money-making**: To make money over the long term, the business must be able to satisfy and retain customers, plus rationalize the most advantageous customer quality and customer base. It must also be able to pay its employees and be a place where employees can expand their personal capacity. Without money-making, the resources to satisfy and retain customers and to rationalize the most advantageous customer quality base and customer base will not be available. Likewise, without money-making, the resources will not be available to pay employees or to expand their personal capacity (so that they can earn pay increases).

- o **Customers**: The business must have customers to generate sales revenue and to have work for employees to do. A business should aim to retain its better customers.

- o **Employees**: Without employees, there is no one to do the work necessary to make money, and to satisfy and retain customers and acquire new customers. A business should aim to retain its better employees.

A good way to think about this is:

**"You cannot have one without the others (at least not for very long)."**

- o If an organization overly focused on money-making, it can lose its customers. Without customers, there will be no future money-making. The business can also lose its best employees, which will be over the long term detrimental to money-making and to satisfying and retaining customers.
- o Over-focusing on customers over time can result in insufficient money-making and in losing the firm's best employees.
- o Insufficient money-making to sustain the organization and losing the firm's customers can result from an over-focus on employees over time. Expenses will become too high to be price competitive and customers will switch to competitors.

**Conclusion**

It is necessary to maintain a balance between money-making, customers, and employees to be a successful business over the long term. The balance is dynamic and ever-changing. It takes considerable skill to create and maintain this balance. But, some companies get it done, and they are the best companies in which to invest, be a customer, and work.

You can observe this easily in the real world. Companies that make money are generally favored by investors. These same companies will generally have very good products and customer service – thereby satisfying and retaining customers; plus, their excellence attracts new customers. Finally, these same companies will generally be great places to work...they will attract the best employees...these companies are the places that people want to work.

Exhibit 6-3

The following is a general financial model that showes some basic financial relationships.  The left side of the model is a very simplified balance sheet, and the right side of the model is a functional format income statement (see Chapter 5).

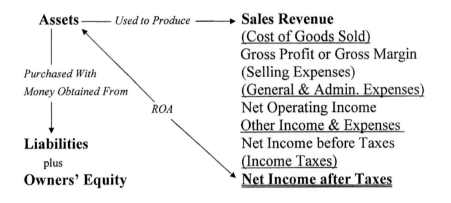

Some important concepts to learn from this model are:

- o  Assets are purchased by either borrowing money (liabilities - finance uses the term debt), or by using the business owners' money (owners' equity).
- o  Both debt and equity have a cost:  lenders charge interest on loans, and stockholders or owners want a return on their investment.  The average cost of the two is the average cost of capital for the business.  The average cost of capital is simply the cost of using the money (the assets):  both debt and equity.
- o  The assets are used to produce sales revenue, which, after all expenses are deducted, hopefully produces a net income after taxes (I call this margin).  This margin is the return on the assets, thus the term "return on assets."
- o  The return on assets should be greater than the cost of capital.  There is no reason to be in business if the company cannot produce a return on its capital (money) greater than the cost of its capital over time.  When the cost of capital is greater than the return on assets, wealth is destroyed.  When the return on assets is greater than the cost of capital, wealth is created.

Appendix 6A

## MIDWEST ALUMINUM, INCORPORATED
### A BUSINESS CASE

### Forward for the Case

The primary purpose of this business case is to give you a sense of what business goals may look like in an actual business situation. The case uses the framework for business goals in Chapter 6 and adds the various activity areas with their respective goals. If the activity areas goals are met, then the overall business goals will be met.

This case also lets you see what an income statement and a balance sheet may look like in the real world. All the numbers that you see are realistic real world numbers. While I have made this business up and made up all the financial information, the case mirrors this company's industry both in general information and financial information.

By studying the business goals and the activity areas goals, you can get a feel for what business managers do and how their performance is evaluated. You will notice that there is a wide range of goals…meaning there is something of interest for just about everyone. For example, say you find that reducing scrap in the plant is interesting and something that you would like to improve…this then is "your thing." Other people might not find that this is "their thing." Another person might really get into developing new products, solving software problems, keeping the promises to employees listed in the business goals, and so on. The idea is to look for what you find interesting, energizing, or exciting…it could become "your thing." What is great about all of this is that organizations will pay you to do "your thing" if it is a need of the organization.

## Midwest Aluminum, Incorporated

Midwest Aluminum, Incorporated is a manufacturer of aluminum windows, doors, and miscellaneous aluminum products for commercial and residential use. The company has one manufacturing plant located in Columbus, Indiana and distribution centers in Columbus, Denver, Atlanta, and Houston. Nancy Hale, currently the Vice President of Operations, and Joe Wilson, currently the Vice President of Marketing, have just purchased the company.

Hale and Wilson have given the previous owner a promissory note for 80% of the company's common stock. The former owner will retain 20% ownership. Hale and Wilson will each own 40% of the company.

### Company History:

Midwest was started in 1976 as a retailer of aluminum windows and doors. The firm began manufacturing operations in 1981, moving to its present plant location in 1995. The plant was expanded in 2001. The retailing business was closed in 1983 to concentrate on manufacturing and the development of a dealer network.

Nancy Hale began working at the company in 1988 as an operations manager after receiving a bachelor's degree in engineering from Purdue University. Since 1988, she has held various positions within the operations area and has held the position of Vice President of Operations since 2003. In addition to her duties at Midwest, Nancy has pursued a vigorous continuing education program. Since 1988, she has received numerous advanced manufacturing and engineering certifications that put her at the cutting edge of her field. It is her objective as an owner/manager to apply advanced manufacturing concepts and techniques that were not allowed by the former owner.

Joe Wilson has been the Vice President of Marketing since 2002. He joined the firm in 1991 as a sales representative working out of the Houston distribution center after receiving his MBA in marketing from Indiana University. In 1993, he became the manager of the

Denver distribution center. He held this position until 1999. At this time, he was promoted to Company Sales Manager and moved to Columbus. Joe holds a bachelor's degree in accounting, and worked for three years in an accounting firm before starting his MBA. While a dedicated marketing professional, Joe still enjoys working with numbers. One of Joe's goals as an owner/manager is to establish an *integrated marketing communications* (IMC) process for the company. IMC is the coordination of all promotional efforts with the objective of producing a unified, customer-focused promotional message.

The company has experienced a period of low profitability in the past seven years. It is this period of low profitability that convinced the former owner to sell the company. The former owner simply lost interest in the company and lost the intense desire necessary to make a business succeed.

In the past seven years, the firm's focus has been shifted from quality to on time delivery to customers, and finally, to the present focus of low cost. The former owner/manager's objective has always been to increase sales revenue. Hale and Wilson believe that the company has no real focus or *distinctive competence* (the thing that a company gets very good at), because of the frequent changes in strategy over the last seven years. The new principals think that managing the company for profitability instead of sales revenue growth and developing a strong distinctive competence will result in improved profitability and prospects for the future.

A continuing problem for the company has been inventory, both slow-moving and obsolete. Both Nancy and Joe agree that products should not be considered "made" until they are sold. Traditional manufacturing practices credit operations with a finished product once it has been made and placed in finished goods inventory. The company has three types of inventory: raw materials inventory, work-in-process inventory, and finished goods inventory. Raw material represents on average 30% of total inventory, work-in-process inventory averages 25%, and finished goods inventory averages 45%.

Two fast growing areas of business in recent years have been windows, doors, and other aluminum products purchased by horse trailer manufacturers, and the manufacture of miscellaneous aluminum products for a variety of business customers. Both product categories are usually custom designed by Midwest's engineering staff, and are produced in batches.

### The Distribution System and Customers:

The company manufactures its products at the Columbus plant. Finished goods are then transported by truck to the Atlanta, Denver, and Houston distribution centers. The average time from completion of manufacturing to the arrival of product at a distribution center is 4.2 days. The Columbus distribution center takes an average of 1 day, Atlanta averages 6 days, Denver averages 7 days, and Houston averages 5 days. The Columbus distribution center is located in a separate building next to the plant. In terms of sales revenue, Columbus accounts for 35% of the firm's sales, Atlanta 20%, Denver 20%, and Houston 25%.

Each of the four distribution centers maintains a sales force that is managed by the company's sales manager. Members of the sales force call on Midwest's customers on a regular basis. Frequently, sales representatives have developed long term relationships with customers. Joe has always believed that quality service is the key to good selling. He believes that he has a solid and dependable sales team. He knows each sales representative personally.

Midwest has five types of customers:
1. Building supply businesses that serve as dealers, for whom the company makes a standard set of products using the *modular* concept. Products are therefore *made-to-stock*. After manufacturing, the products are placed in finished goods inventory and sent to a distribution center. Dealer orders are then filled from this inventory. An advantage to this type of business is that products are manufactured to the firm's sales forecast, allowing for efficient scheduling and production. A

disadvantage is that the firm has an inventory carrying cost, which averages 25% per year of the carried inventory.

2. Large construction companies that buy in volume directly from Midwest, for whom the company will design and manufacture products to the customer's specifications. This is called *make-to-order*. An advantage of this business is that the company does not carry any finished goods inventory, since once the products are produced they are shipped directly to the customer. A disadvantage is that the planning and scheduling of manufacturing becomes more difficult.

3. Manufacturers of manufactured buildings that purchase the company's products as components of their products. These customers typically purchase large quantities of product that Midwest designs and builds to the customer's specifications. Again, an advantage is that the firm has no finished goods inventory carrying costs.

4. Manufacturers of horse trailers that buy products designed and manufactured to their specifications. Quantities can range from small to large, depending on the customer and the product.

5. Firms purchasing custom designed and manufactured aluminum products. The volumes can go from small to large depending on the product. For these products, the company typically collects a 50% deposit before production and the remaining 50% after delivery.

**Company Credit Policies:**

Midwest attempts to collect its *accounts receivables* in 30 days. It offers an early payment discount of 1% if the customer pays within 10 days of billing. The company's billing system takes 7 days to generate a bill after the product is delivered. Interest is not charged until an account is more than 60 days past due. Presently, the firm does not have a full time credit manager, instead relying on members of the accounting department to complete credit and collection tasks.

**Employees:**
The current labor market in Columbus is good for hiring employees. Experienced people are available. Overtime costs Midwest 1.5 times regular time. Hiring costs are currently $1,700 per employee, and firing/layoff costs are $2,300 per employee.

**Competition and the Environment:**
Customers are now expecting more quality at a lower cost. Competitors have attempted to differentiate their product in various ways. Some competitors have tried lowest cost, while others have concentrated on performance and quality. A few have tried flexibility (making any size or style that the customer wants). On-time delivery is always important to customers, as they have production schedules of their own to meet.

### The New Owner/Managers

Nancy and Joe's first few weeks in control of the company have been busy ones. As a near-term focus, the principals believe that they can increase profitability and stabilize the business financially by focusing on three primary things:
1. Eliminating unprofitable customers
2. Redesigning, repositioning, or eliminating unprofitable products
3. Paying each position (employee) in the company the fair market value for that position

The new owner/managers have determined the following business goals:

### The Business Goals for Midwest Aluminum, Incorporated
1. Sales revenue goal: operate ahead of the curve with a 12 month rolling forecast that has a control process in place to make needed adjustments to operating plans in a quick, timely manner. The

sales revenue goal for the next 12 months is $27,952,000 using average operating assets of $4,834,000.
2. Gross margin goal: 23.66% of sales revenue
3. Net income before taxes goal: 2.74% of sales revenue
4. Successfully introduce three new products in the next 12 months that are producing 3.12% of the company's sales revenue by month 12.
5. Shift 22.7% of customers up one grade rank in customer quality
6. Keep this promise: Each employee will be rewarded for the value that they add to the company.

To accomplish the business goals outlined above, the owner/managers have created teams with goals. The teams are divided by activity areas.

**Operations Activity - Team Goals:**
1. Reduce material costs by 0.5%
2. Develop a quality control system and a system to calculate cost of quality
3. Reduce product scrap from 0.6% to 0.4%
4. Improve on time order delivery to 90%
5. Decrease product returns to 0.6% of sales
6. Establish a supplier ranking system
7. Reduce raw material and work-in-process inventory at the plant by 28.6%

**Marketing Activity - Team Goals:**
1. Increase existing customer profitability by 1.3% per year
2. Develop a customer evaluation system to determine customer quality
3. Develop a customer base evaluation system
4. Develop a plan to improve brand awareness in the company's target markets
5. Establish an IMC (Integrated Marketing Communications) process and budget

6. Target three new products in a 12 month period
7. Reduce slow-moving and obsolete inventory by 31.7%

**Finance Activity – Team Goals:**
1. Develop detailed information on the company's capital structure
2. Develop strategies to reduce the firm's average cost of debt
3. Develop strategies to improve the company's current ratio and acid test ratio
4. Do a financial analysis on updating the company's manufacturing equipment
5. Do a financial analysis on adding automation upgrades to current manufacturing equipment
6. Calculate the Net Present Value (NPV) of new products developed by marketing

**Accounting Activity – Team Goals:**
1. Assist the owner/managers in developing a 12 month rolling forecast with a control process that can make quick and timely adjustments to the business plan.
2. Develop detailed information on the firm's cost structure
3. Provide the operations team with detailed manufacturing cost information
4. Provide the marketing team with detailed marketing cost information
5. Provide the marketing team with detailed customer revenue and cost information
6. Provide the HR team with cost information on each employee in the company
7. Assist the owner/managers in developing a plan to increase the firm's cash account

**Human Resources Activity – Team Goals:**
1. Improve overall worker protection by reducing job-related medical claims to 21 (there were 37 claims in 2007) during the next 12 months
2. Identify employment requirements for the next three years

3. Develop a model employee profile
4. Decide the wage structure for the firm and the current fair market value for each position
5. Create a system for evaluating employees
6. Reduce employee turnover: reduce new hires per year from 38 to 30 and reduce firings from 15 to 10 during the next 12 months
7. Reduce people cost as a percentage of sales revenue to 21.31% (was 22.4% in 2007)

**Information Systems Activity – Team Goals:**
1. Assist all areas in the reduction of people cost as a percentage of sales revenue, net operating income, and margin by using more information technology
2. Support managers with new inventory control software
3. Resolve the software needs of the sales force
4. Work with accounting to update accounting software
5. Ensure that all areas of the business use compatible hardware and software

Exhibit 1     MIDWEST ALUMINUM, INCORPORATED
Income statement
For the Calendar Year 2007

| | | |
|---|---|---|
| Sales Revenue | $28,262,185 | |
| Returns | (262,112) | |
| Net Sales | $28,000,073 | 100.00% |
| | | |
| *Cost of Goods Sold* | | |
| Material | 17,778,230 | |
| Labor | 2,595,932 | |
| Supervision | 558,078 | |
| Supplies | 171,546 | |
| Maintenance Expense | 125,278 | |
| Payroll Taxes | 239,714 | |
| Depreciation | 147,550 | |
| Utilities | 110,631 | |
| Lease Expense | 403,897 | |
| | | |
| Cost of Goods Sold | (22,130,856) | 79.04% |
| Gross Margin | 5,869,217 | 20.96% |
| | | |
| *Selling Expenses* | | |
| Salaries | 1,588,783 | |
| Commissions | 0 | |
| Payroll Taxes | 120,624 | |
| Sales Travel | 129,138 | |
| Sales Promotion | 41,747 | |
| Trucking Expense | 752,157 | |
| Advertising | 6,714 | |
| Depreciation | 40,346 | |
| | | |
| Selling Expenses | (2,679,509) | 9.57% |

*General & Administrative Expenses*

| | | |
|---|---|---|
| Salaries and Payroll Taxes | 1,228,214 | |
| Office & Computer Supplies | 56,079 | |
| Insurance | 253,794 | |
| Misc Taxes | 86,976 | |
| Depreciation | 72,614 | |
| Bad Debts Expense | 95,195 | |
| G & A Travel | 28,448 | |
| Employee Health Care | 588,953 | |
| Other Expenses | 384,862 | |
| General & Administrative Expenses | (2,795,135) | 9.98% |
| Net Operating Income | 394,573 | 1.41% |

*Other Income and Expense*

| | | |
|---|---|---|
| Interest Expense | 207,634 | |
| Interest Income | (366) | |
| Gain/Loss on Sale of Fixed Assets | (5,852) | |
| Other Income and Expense | (201,416) | 0.72% |
| Net Income Before Taxes | 193,157 | 0.69% |
| Income Taxes (28% tax rate) | (54,084) | 0.19% |
| Net Income After Taxes | $139,073 | 0.50% |

Exhibit 2     MIDWEST ALUMINUM, INCORPORATEI
Balance Sheet
December 31, 2007

*Current Assets*

| | | |
|---|---|---|
| Cash | $ 157,576 | |
| Accounts Receivable-Net(1) | 2,029,480 | |
| Inventory | 1,954,176 | |
| Current Assets | $4,141,232 | 75.88% |
| Fixed Assets-Net of Depreciation | 1,147,824 | 21.03% |
| Other Assets | 168,796 | 3.09% |
| TOTAL ASSETS | $5,457,852 | 100.00% |

*Current Liabilities*

| | | |
|---|---|---|
| Short-term Loans & Current Maturities | 983,920 | |
| Accounts Payable | 1,845,823 | |
| Current Liabilities | 2,829,743 | 51.85% |
| Long-term Debt less Current Maturities | 961,835 | 17.62% |
| TOTAL LIABILITIES | 3,791,578 | 69.47% |
| TOTAL STOCKHOLDERS' EQUITY | 1,666,274 | 30.53% |
| TOTAL LIABILITIES & STOCKHOLDERS' EQUITY | $5,457,852 | 100.00% |

Footnotes:

(1) Accounts Receivable less Allowance for Doubtful Accounts of $50,000

# CHAPTER 7

## *Operations*

In the next three chapters (7, 8, and 9), I am going to focus on the three functional areas of a business: operations, marketing, and finance. I will start with the operations function.

### What is Operations?

Operations is the part of an organization that produces the product. Remember from page one of the book that I am using the word "product" to mean either a physical good or service, or a combination of the two. At first, it might appear that the production of physical goods is quite different from the delivery of services. In reality both involve the transformation of inputs into outputs. Thus, the term *operations* can refer to either the production of physical goods or the production of services, which I will simply call "products." Sometimes people call operations "production." This term implies that the company makes physical goods.

People involved in business need to have an understanding of modern operations methods because every business produces some type of product. For a business to be successful, it must serve customers well. Invariably, serving customers well means delivering excellent quality in a timely manner, and doing so at the lowest possible cost.

*Operations management is all about designing and operating production methods that are quick, consistent, and inexpensive.*

People work to create firms that are effective and efficient. **Effectiveness** is doing the things that result in the most value creation for the company. **Efficiency** is doing something at the lowest possible cost. The relationship between value and cost is called the *value ratio*. If a firm can provide a better product at the same price, the value ratio will improve for the customer. If the firm can provide a better product at a lower price, then the value ratio will go way up. Studying operations management can teach us how intelligent and skilled management can achieve high levels of value relative to cost for customers.

Operations takes inputs and, using its conversion process (also called transformation process), creates outputs. Examples of inputs and outputs are shown below. The conversion process is simply doing that thing that the company does. For example, if the company makes cars, it has a conversion process to convert inputs into cars.

| **Inputs** | | **Outputs** |
|---|---|---|
| Energy | | |
| Materials | | Physical Goods |
| Labor  ➜ | **CONVERSION PROCESS**  ➜ | Services |
| Information | | Satisfied Customers |
| Capital | | |

The objective of operations management is for the value created in this conversion process to exceed its cost. For business, this means that the cost of the inputs and conversion needs to be less than the value of the products created. Customers will purchase the product when the customer's ratio of value to cost, or value ratio, becomes favorable enough in their eyes.

The operations conversion process must interact with and is affected by its external environment. The external environment consists of such things as government, competitors, society, and customers - anything that is external to the conversion process.

**Some Examples of Inputs and Outputs:**
- o A restaurant has inputs of food, energy, service staff, equipment, cooks, and knowledge of the restaurant business. These inputs are converted into meals, service, and satisfied customers.
- o A construction business has inputs of concrete, steel, wood products, finish products, labor, equipment, energy, and knowledge that are converted into completed buildings and satisfied clients.
- o Some of the inputs for a university are buildings, faculty, staff, and information. The university converts these inputs into public service, educated students, and research.
- o Inputs for a hospital include buildings, equipment, doctors, medicine, nurses, staff, energy, and supplies. Outputs include healthy patients and public service.

### Operations Decisions

A good way to begin thinking about operations is to develop an understanding of the four main categories of decisions that are made by operations managers. These four categories are:

- o **PROCESS** decisions are about how to make the product. This could include the facility (building), the physical method used for production, and workforce practices. Organizations have found that developing superior processes can be a powerful competitive weapon. Frequently, competitors can purchase a company's product and easily copy it. But copying a firm's processes is difficult and time consuming at best.

- o **QUALITY** systems are used to manage and control the quality of the output of the conversion process. The objective of a quality system is to reduce the variability of the output. Meaning, each unit of output is the same as the last unit. Variability is the enemy of quality. In operations, quality is making the product to specifications. The product specifications are generally derived by marketing from the marketplace…marketing seeks to understand a target market (a group of potential customers), and specifications for a product are developed to reach that target market (more on target markets in the next chapter on marketing).

o **CAPACITY** decisions seek to have the right amount of capacity in the right place at the right time. Capacity is how much can be produced in a given time period. For example, if a restaurant has a grill that can cook 100 hamburgers per hour, then we could say that the restaurant has a maximum capacity of 100 hamburgers per hour. It is not possible for the restaurant to make more than 100 hamburgers in one hour without either adding a second grill or replacing the old grill with a larger one. Capacity defines the maximum output of the conversion process. A firm wants to have enough capacity to satisfy its customers, but not too much capacity since it is expensive to purchase and maintain. Generally, a company's goal is to have just enough capacity, so that it can both satisfy its customers and offer competitive prices.

o **INVENTORY** consists of three types of inventory: raw material inventory, work-in-process inventory, and finished goods inventory. *Raw material inventory* decisions relate to what raw materials to order and how and when to order them. Raw material includes all the materials that the company uses to make its product. One company's finished product can be another company's raw material. *Finished goods inventory* decisions are about how much inventory is needed to achieve the firm's desired service level. *Service level* is the percentage of time that a company can fill customer orders from inventory. The quantity of *work-in-process inventory* will be strongly affected by the type of conversion process used and by the production scheduling methods.

### Types of Processes

In Chapter 3 on Management, a process was defined as a series of activities necessary to complete a task. While there are many names for processes and variations of processes, processes can generally be placed into one of three categories:

- **LINE** processes are characterized by a linear sequence of activities. Step #1 is completed before Step #2. Step #2 is completed before Step #3, and so on. The output moves from one step to the next, in order, from beginning to end. An example is a vehicle assembly line. Line processes are capable of producing large amounts of product with low per-unit product costs. Output variety is generally low. When customers do not need or want product variety, but instead want high volumes of product, low product price, and high product quality, organizations will usually choose the line process.

- **BATCH** processes produce in lots or batches. Batches move from work center to work center in a jumbled sequence. A work center is a group of similar machines or processes. Examples of work centers are a work center for grinding, a work center for painting, and a work center for welding. Batch processes are typically used when medium volumes of product are needed...meaning there is not enough demand for the product for a line process to be efficient. Batch processes can make a large variety of products. Because of the jumbled sequencing of work center activity, batch processes are generally difficult to schedule efficiently, but still remain the best choice for most companies for medium volumes of production.

- **PROJECT** is a form of operations that makes a unique or one-of-a-kind output. Examples are buildings, large ships, and movies. Because the output has never been made before, projects are characterized by difficult planning and scheduling. Cost control can also be very difficult. Project processes are very good at producing high variety. Per-unit product costs will likely be higher than those of batch or line processes.

The following table summarizes the basic characteristics of line, batch, and project processes:

| *Characteristic* | *Line* | *Batch* | *Project* |
|---|---|---|---|
| **Product:** | | | |
| Order Type | Large Batch or Continuous | Batch | Single Unit |
| Volume | High | Medium | Single Unit |
| Product Variety | Low | High | Very High |
| Flow of Product | Sequenced | Jumbled | Sequenced |
| **Labor:** | | | |
| Pay | Lower | Higher | Higher |
| Skills | Lower | Higher | Higher |
| Task Type | Repetitive | Varied | Highly Varied |
| **Capital:** | | | |
| Investment | Higher | Medium | Lower |
| Equipment Used | Special Purpose | General Purpose | General Purpose |
| Inventory Levels | Lower | Higher | Little |

## Why Are There Different Types of Processes?

Each type of process has advantages in producing certain types of products and volumes of those products. The processes used should be the ones that will get the job done with the lowest per-unit product cost. Customers don't really care about the process used - the customer is focused on the outcome: the value of the product and its price (the value ratio discussed earlier in this chapter).

## The Primary Objectives of Operations

A second way to think and learn about operations is to become familiar with the primary objectives of operations:

o **COST** means that the firm strives to have the lowest price. This implies that the firm must maintain low cost operations and marketing.

o **QUALITY** entails that the products produced by the firm are "fit for use" by the customer. The variability of the firm's outputs are kept to a minimum. The firm seeks to have superior quality compared to that of competitors.

o **FLEXIBILITY** is the ability to make whatever the customer wants. For example, the firm can paint the product any color that the buyer would like - this would be high flexibility. Flexibility also means things like how fast a company can introduce new products, or how fast it can adjust its capacity by a certain percentage.

o **DELIVERY** is about being able to deliver the completed product when promised (Reliability), or to make it fast (Speed). Examples are one-hour photo developing, or a 15 minute oil change for your car.

o **INNOVATION** is designing and making products that are new to the marketplace.

Operations objectives can be stated in quantitative and measurable terms. A company should have a goal five years (usually 5 to 10 years) into the future, and also compare its current performance with that of its world-class competitor. The world-class competitor is currently the best in the world, in the same industry as the company. Here are some examples of five year goals:

| | Current Year | Goal: 5 Years into the Future | Current World-Class Competitor |
|---|---|---|---|
| **Cost:** | | | |
| -Inventory turnover | 6.2 | 7.1 | 7.0 |
| -Manufacturing cost as a percentage of sales | 55.5% | 52.0% | 51.1% |
| | | | |
| **Quality:** | | | |
| -Warranty cost as a percentage of sales | 1% | 0.5% | 0.75% |
| -Customer satisfaction | 88% | 95% | 92% |
| | | | |
| **Flexibility:** | | | |
| -Number of months to introduce a new product | 12 months | 6 months | 10 months |
| | | | |
| **Delivery:** | | | |
| -Percentage of orders filled from stock | 95% | 96% | 94% |
| -Lead time | 25 days | 19 days | 25 days |
| | | | |
| **Innovation:** | | | |
| -Number of product innovations per year (first-to-market) | 2 | 3 | 2 |

### Operations Objectives and the Customer

A business should focus on one of the primary operations objectives. This objective is the main reason the customer buys a product from the seller. The organization seeks to execute this operations objective better than any of its competitors. For example, if a firm's main operations objective is quality, then the firm would concentrate on making higher quality products than its rivals. The other operations objectives would become qualifiers. The business must execute its qualifiers well enough to "qualify" the firm for consideration by customers. This generally means doing these operations objectives at the industry standard (at least as well as competitors). Qualifiers cannot by themselves earn a sale. However, unacceptable performance on the qualifiers can lose the sale. The primary operations objective is what earns the customer's business. Let's use Wal-Mart as an example. Wal-Mart's main operations objective is low cost. People go to Wal-Mart because of its low prices.

## Supply Chain Management

The main idea of supply chain management is to use a total system approach to manage the flow of materials and information from raw material suppliers, to factories, to warehouses, and to the final customer. While called a chain, the supply chain is actually a network of suppliers, manufacturers, distributors, and retailers. The network is managed as a system to coordinate activities between members and to maximize overall efficiency of the network.

A primary focus of supply chain management is to eliminate waste within the network. Operations managers at the company level seek to make the ratio of value to cost more favorable by reducing waste in the operations. **Waste** is any activity that does not add value to the product or service. Likewise, supply chains are managed with waste elimination in mind. The elimination of waste results in lower costs, less time to make products, and improved quality. Reducing waste increases efficiency. Improved efficiency will generally improve the ratio of value to cost, thereby making the product more attractive to customers.

Why would a company want to participate in a supply chain? For a firm to be a member of a supply chain, it must be to the firm's advantage to do so. Thus, one of the characteristics of a supply chain is that all participants must be better off because of their network participation.

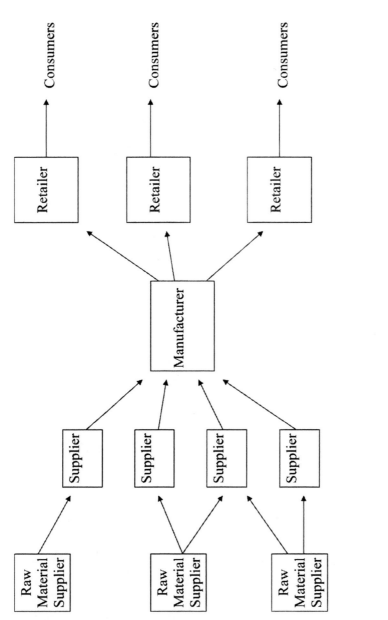

Exhibit 7-1: An example of a very simple supply chain network

In some cases, firms must be in supply chains to be competitive in the modern marketplace. Without the efficiencies created by supply chains, a firm may find that its costs are too high, production time too long, or product quality too low, leaving it unable to successfully compete with its rivals.

Remember that the consumer is usually not concerned with the details of production. Consumers are primarily focused on the outcome: the product's value and its price. Supply chain management seeks to produce the product desired by the consumer at the lowest total delivered cost to the consumer. To best accomplish this goal, it is necessary for suppliers, manufacturers, distributors, and retailers to work together to eliminate waste that increases cost and delivery time.

Take a minute to look at Exhibit 7-1: an example of a very simple supply chain network. Materials move from left to right, starting in this example with raw material suppliers, then to the suppliers, to the manufacturer, to retailers, and finally to consumers. Depending on a firm's position in the supply chain, everything to its left is upstream (its source of supply) and everything to its right is downstream (its distribution channel). Just think of water flowing in a river…the water always flows in one direction…in a supply chain, so do materials. In contrast, information flows both upstream and downstream in the supply chain network. Good information flow is critical for a supply chain to function efficiently. For example, the retailer is collecting information on what consumers are purchasing today. Members of the supply chain need to know this…what consumers are buying. Adjustments can then be made immediately – changes in colors, changes in styles, etc., because the information flow is electronic and therefore fast.

### The Differences between Physical Goods and Services

Physical goods are easy to recognize, but services can be tricky. Most definitions of service stress the intangibility of the product. Another definition is that a service is produced and consumed simultaneously. The service never exists; it is the results of the service that are observable. The fact that the service is produced and consumed at the same time is important because this implies that the customer must be in the production system during production. The customer's presence can introduce uncertainty into the production system by placing demands on the producer at the time of production. The following table compares service and physical goods:

| Service | Physical Goods |
|---|---|
| Does not exist before purchase | Can be demonstrated and examined before purchase |
| Cannot be stored in inventory | Can be stored in inventory |
| Intangible | Tangible |
| No resale is possible | Resale is possible |
| Cannot be returned if customer is dissatisfied | Can be returned for refund |
| Cannot be transported (although producers can be) | Can be transported |
| Production and consumption are simultaneous | Production and consumption can be spatially separated |
| Sales and production cannot be separated functionally | Sales and production can be separated functionally |
| Production units must be located close to the customer | Production units need not be close to the customer |
| Buyer takes part in production and can even perform part of the production | Seller produces |

Service can be described as a simultaneous marketing and operations act. Therefore, close coordination of marketing and operations is necessary for successful design and delivery of services. In many cases, it becomes difficult to tell what is marketing and what is operations, because the two become so intertwined in services.

## Products Usually Consist of Both Physical Goods and Services

Most products actually come to the buyer as a bundle of physical goods and services. For example, the consumer purchases a new TV (the physical good), but included in the sales price is a product warranty (a service). Understanding the bundle of physical goods and services is helpful in understanding how sellers create value in the marketplace. For consumers, it helps in understanding exactly what we are buying…it helps us understand what is important to us when purchasing products. The bundle of physical goods and services consists of three main elements:

o **The Physical Goods**: in the TV example above, this is the TV; this includes the plastic, the metal, the screws, the knobs, etc.

o **The Tangible Service** is easy to remember; just think of the senses. This would be the sight, sound, feel, and smell that the customer experiences. With a TV, this would be the sight of the picture, the sound from its speakers, etc. There would also be some tangible service during the buying experience.

o **The Psychological Service** encompasses such things as the buyer being comfortable that there will not be any problems or hassles during the purchasing experience. That the physical goods will perform as promised, and that the tangible service will be pleasant. In the TV example, this is the warranty as well as things like the reputation of the seller (both the retailer and the manufacturer). A big thing here is trust…the buyer must trust the seller.

What the customer is purchasing is a mix of physical goods, tangible services, and psychological services. It is important in designing a bundle of physical goods and services not to overemphasize the physical goods and the sensual service. The key factor is to properly read the customers' needs and expectations, and then to provide the proper mix in the bundle. *Frequently, the psychological service is very important to the buyer.* Its importance should not be underestimated for many, many products.

## Some Important Operations Concepts

### Bottleneck

The bottleneck is the slowest part of an operation. It limits the capacity of the process. Refer back to the restaurant example in the capacity section, in which a restaurant had a grill capable of making a maximum of 100 hamburgers per hour. Suppose the restaurant served only hamburgers, could seat 250 people, could serve 250 people with drinks and other meal accompaniments, and that each customer spent one hour at the restaurant and ate exactly one hamburger. The bottleneck would then be the grill, as only 100 hamburgers could be made per hour, resulting in the restaurant being able to serve only 100 people per hour. The extra seating and service capacity would go unused. Efficiency for the overall system would be reduced, resulting in higher costs per customer.

### Setup Time

Setup time refers to the time it takes to switch from making one product to making another. Setup time does not add value to the product. Setup time is therefore considered waste. Reducing setup time lowers waste and also improves the organization's flexibility, as the firm can switch from product to product faster. Fast setup times eliminate the need for long production runs or large batches. The planning and scheduling of the operations is made much easier.

### Uptime Percentage

Uptime percentage is the percentage of time that the production system is operating correctly. When machines break, there are material shortages, or any number of things that happen to disrupt production – this is called downtime. Downtime is waste since it does not add value to the product. As an example, if machines were broken 4 hours in a 40 hour work week, downtime would be 10% (4 hours divided by 40 hours) and uptime would be 90% (36 hours divided by 40 hours). Improving the uptime percentage is critical to good operations and serving customers well.

### Throughput

Throughput is the number of units of product that the production system produces in a given time period. The goal is to increase throughput. A common goal in business is to reduce labor costs as a percentage of revenue. Increasing throughput will help accomplish this goal. Remember that working harder will not get this done...working smarter is the way to increase throughput. A more sensitive measure of labor costs is labor cost as a percentage of margin (sales revenue minus expenses equals margin).

### Scrap

Scrap is the cost of labor and material for product that cannot be used or sold. The goal is to reduce scrap. Savings in scrap will go directly to profit, so even small reductions in scrap can make a big difference. Reduction in scrap is particularly important when the materials used in making the product are expensive, or where labor costs per hour are expensive.

### Productivity

Productivity is a measure of how well a country, industry, or organization is using its resources. Productivity is a relative measure; in other words, to be meaningful, it must be compared to something else. Business firms typically compare their performance with the performance of their competitors using a process called *benchmarking*.

To raise productivity:
o   Increase outputs while inputs remain constant
o   Outputs remain constant while inputs are lowered
o   Increase outputs and lower inputs at the same time

Productivity is lowered when:
o   Outputs decrease while inputs remain constant
o   Outputs remain constant while inputs increase
o   Outputs decrease and inputs increase at the same time

## Product Design and New Products

Organizations desire to introduce new products because new products provide growth opportunities and can gain a competitive advantage for the firm over its competitors. Businesses with the ability to successfully introduce profitable new products typically are more profitable and have a higher potential for growth.

In the modern business world, there is the challenge to introduce new products faster without any loss of quality. In recent years, firms have been able to lower product introduction times to mere fractions of previous years. One of the reasons this competency has become so important is that product life cycles are shortening. This means that products remain profitable in the marketplace for increasingly shorter periods of time before they are replaced by a newer, more advanced product offering. There are three basic ways to design and introduce new products:

o **Technology or Production Push** is the view that technology or production is the main determinant of the products that the firm should design, introduce, and make. There is little regard for the market; instead, the firm develops superior technologies or production methods and products. The products are then "pushed" into the market and marketing's job is to create demand for these superior products. The idea is that since the products are superior, an advantage is created and customers will want to purchase the products.

o **Market Pull** is the view that the market is the primary method for determining new products with little consideration of technology. The firm should make what it can sell. Customer needs are determined. Then the company organizes the resources and processes required to design and make an offering to supply the customer. Thus, the market "pulls" products into the marketplace.

o The **Integrated Method** holds that the product should both fit market needs and have a technological or production advantage. This way is the most difficult to implement, but also the most appealing. If it can be successfully implemented, this way will usually produce the best results.

## New Themes in Operations

### Time Reduction
Organizations are dramatically reducing the time it takes to make products. This time is called **lead-time**. Reducing lead-time results in a host of benefits, including the need for less working capital to operate the organization, shortened forecasting periods, and lower inventory levels for a given service level. Shortened lead-time will increase a firm's flexibility.

### Continuous Improvement
The modern world demands that both individuals and organizations be in a state of continuous improvement. Continuous improvement is a way of life and a way of being in business. Continuous improvement in business is the constant search for how to serve the customer better, at a lower price.

### The Environment
Today, business and consumers must help protect the environment. Progressive companies are finding that reducing pollution can pay. Superior processes pollute less and can also reduce the cost of the product through less wasted material. Thus, pollution costs and material costs can be reduced.

### Globalization of Operations
Global corporations operate on a global basis. Operations decisions are not made on a country-by-country basis or a region-by-region basis,

but rather on a global basis. Factories are located based on worldwide requirements. The best suppliers in the world are sought as suppliers for the global corporation. Processes are standardized throughout the world. Variations in products for specific market segments or geographic areas are considered options rather than different products.

## Technology

Managers must concentrate on the performance characteristics of technologies. By doing so, managers need not be masters of the intricacies of technologies, but will still be able to make the appropriate decisions relating to technology choice and operation.

## Developing Trends in Operations Technology

o *Robots and Robotics* are programmable machines that perform repetitive tasks.

o *Computer Aided Design (CAD)* is the use of computers to aid in design engineering activities. Cost reductions are obtained with the improvement in productivity and the accuracy in drafting new designs.

o *Computer Integrated Manufacturing (CIM)* uses computer systems to integrate product design, material flow, and production. CIM ensures that the firm has the facilities and capability to manufacture new product designs.

o *Flexible Manufacturing Systems (FMS)* are computer-controlled systems of programmable machine tools. Production methods can be modified quickly via computer.

## Some Measures of Internal Business Process Performance

Let's take a brief look at how to measure the performance of business processes.

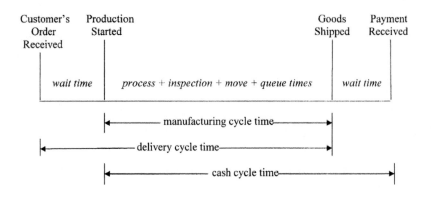

<u>Value-Added Time</u>
Process Time

<u>Non-Value-Added Time</u>
Wait Time
Inspection Time
Move Time
Queue Time

**Manufacturing cycle time** (throughput) is the amount of time that it takes to convert raw materials into finished products. Manufacturing cycle time can be broken into four categories:

o **Process time:** the time when work is being done on the product…**only process time adds value to the product**

o **Inspection time:** the time that is used making sure that the product is not defective

o **Move time:** the time spent moving either partially completed products from work station to work station or finished products from an assembly line to finished goods inventory

o **Queue time:** the time that the product spends waiting to be worked on, inspected, moved, or shipped

**Delivery cycle time** is the time between when the customer's order is received and when the finished product is shipped.

**Cash cycle time** is the time it takes from the start of production (when we start to put money into the product) to when we receive payment for the product.

### Manufacturing cycle efficiency

Some companies have been able to lower the manufacturing cycle time to a mere fraction of its previous level. This is accomplished by eliminating non-value-added activities: inspection, moving, and queuing. In some cases, lowering the manufacturing cycle time and lowering the wait time after the receipt of the customer's order has resulted in reducing delivery cycle time from months to weeks or sometimes even months to hours. We can calculate manufacturing cycle efficiency:

*Manufacturing cycle efficiency = Process time ÷ Manufacturing cycle time*

A manufacturing cycle efficiency of less than one (1.0) means that there is non-value-added time in the production system. For example, .40 would mean that 60% of a product's time would be spent in non-value-added activities. In many manufacturing companies, the manufacturing cycle efficiency is less than .10 (10%). So, why all the fuss about manufacturing cycle efficiency? Reducing non-value-added activities means that the seller can get the product into the hands of the customer faster (and get paid sooner), and do so at a lower cost.

### Summary

OK, so now we have a good summary of operations. Try to think about operations from the perspective of the four main operations decisions (your operations framework): process, quality, capacity, and inventory. This will make it easier to learn more about operations and to make sense out of what you already know. Now that we have learned about how products are made, it is time to turn our attention to selling products – marketing.

# CHAPTER 8

## *Marketing*

**What Is Marketing?**

Marketing provides operations with the needed direction to make sure the products that are produced are those that are desired by the customer. Once the products are produced (the output), marketing must make sure that they find their way to the right customer. This is a much broader definition than the notion that marketing's job is to sell the product. Marketing must first determine what customers want or need, meaning what products are likely to sell well. Then the customers' wants and needs must be converted into an *offering* – the product that the firm intends to sell. Operations will then make the offering. Marketing takes the completed output and seeks to get it into the hands of customers that want or need the output. The key factor is **customer satisfaction**, which is the extent that a firm fulfills a customers' needs, wants, and expectations.

While this broad definition of marketing is important to get a sense of the scope of marketing, the main concern in a business is sales revenue. Sales revenue is the driver of cash flow, and cash flow is critical to staying in business and being competitive as a seller. Therefore, marketing pays the most attention to selling, since selling is what is required to generate sales revenue. A part of selling is how to get to market – meaning how to link the seller and the buyer – this linking consists primarily of promotion and distribution. We will cover both promotion and distribution in this chapter.

### Utility

Utility is the ability of a product to satisfy a human need or want. There are several types of utility:

- **Form** utility is the process of forming inputs into the desired outputs.
- **Task** utility is provided when someone performs a task for someone else.
- **Time** utility is having the output available for sale at the time it is wanted by the customer.
- **Place** utility is having the output available for sale where the customer wants it.
- **Possession** utility is being able to transfer ownership to the customer at the time of purchase. This means that the customer has the right to use or consume the product. Customers usually exchange money for possession utility.

Form and task utilities are the responsibility of operations, and must be something that customers need or want, or no utility can be created. After operations has completed form and/or task utility, customers will still not be satisfied until marketing provides time, place, and possession utility.

### Why Marketing Is Important To You

Marketing is important to every individual because each of us is a consumer. Everyone purchases and uses products to live and function in the world. Knowledge of marketing is an important part of being a good consumer, as each of us will be dealing with marketing (Time, Place, and Possession Utility) for our entire lives.

As consumers, we pay for the cost of marketing activities. In advanced economies, marketing costs average about 50 cents of each consumer dollar. Many people are surprised to learn that the production (form utility) of the product represents only about half of their consumer dollar. For example, winter boots made in Texas are only of use to someone in Indiana when the boots are in Indiana (place utility). Winter boots are most desired by customers in Indiana in the wintertime (time utility). And finally, people in Indiana must have the right to use the winter boots (possession utility) that are made by the firm in Texas. Each of the four types of utility must be present to create a satisfied customer. The absence of one of the types of utility will result in an unsatisfied customer: winter boots that leak, winter boots in Florida when the customer is in Indiana, winter boots in Indiana in the summer when the customer wanted them in the winter, winter boots in the warehouse but not available for possession transfer, and so on.

Effective marketing is needed to link producers and consumers. Marketing links sellers and buyers. Without marketing, we as consumers would have difficulty finding the products that we want. And sellers would have difficulty finding buyers for their products. This would result in inefficiency, which over time would increase prices. So, while about 50 cents (on average) of each consumer dollar goes toward marketing, this expenditure results in an overall reduction in the prices we pay because of the efficiency generated by effective marketing.

### A Brief History of Business and Marketing

Up until the 1920s, our country was in what is called the *production era*. During this time, demand for products exceeded the supply. Sellers were just beginning to understand how to produce products efficiently. As a result, there were not a lot of products produced in relation to the demand. Therefore, sellers could sell just about anything that they made. Sellers focused on increasing output and efficiency. The prevailing attitude was, "a good product will sell itself."

By the 1920s, production was beginning to become more efficient. The production of products began to exceed the demand.

Sellers realized that to sell their offerings, they had to do something besides just make the product. This reality resulted in the *sales era*, where companies began active selling efforts. Competition between sellers was increasing. Firms focused on making products that they thought customers would want, and marketing promoted products by advertising, enlarging sales forces, taking orders, and delivering products. A prevailing attitude was, "creative advertising and selling will overcome consumers' resistance and convince them to buy."

By the 1950s, the operations function was becoming more efficient. The supply of products exceeded demand. Organizations could see that selling efforts were not enough to ensure success. The *marketing era* began. This is also called the **marketing concept**. The marketing concept is a business philosophy that involves the entire organization in satisfying customer needs, while at the same time achieving organizational goals. Another way to think about this is the organization aims all its efforts at satisfying customer needs and doing so at a profit. All areas of the business are viewed as playing a part in satisfying customer needs. The prevailing attitude is, "the customer is king! Find a need and fill that need."

**The marketing concept is basically a three-step process:**
o   Assess the needs of potential customers for products
o   Develop a product (offering) to satisfy these needs
o   Continue to seek ways to provide customer satisfaction

During this time, business managers realized that they were not in business to produce physical goods and services, but rather were in business to satisfy customer needs.

An extension of the marketing concept occurred in the 1990s with the *relationship era*. **Relationship marketing** strives to develop mutually beneficial relationships between the buyer and the seller. These relationships are generally thought of as longer-term in nature, seek to stimulate customer loyalty, and of course, enhance customer satisfaction. Examples are grocery discount cards and frequent flyer miles with airlines. The prevailing attitude is, "long-term relationships with customers and other partners lead to success."

Relationship marketing is a shift from traditional transaction-based marketing. With transaction-based marketing, marketing is considered a simple exchange process. The goal is to identify prospective buyers, convert them to customers, and complete sales transactions. This is a short-term view of a simple exchange process; however, the concept of relationship marketing is much more complex and longer-term in nature, as described above. The idea of relationship marketing is partly related to new information technologies. Firms have the tools today to develop certain relationships, whereas in the past, the tools were not available.

## Markets

### Production Orientation and Marketing Orientation

A manager with a production orientation focuses on products that are easier for the firm to make, and then tries to sell them. This orientation entails thinking that customers exist to purchase the firm's outputs.

A marketing-oriented manager thinks that the firm exists to serve customers well, and in a broader sense, to fill the needs of society. A marketing orientation means working to carry out the marketing concept.

### Converting Needs to Wants

By concentrating on the product's benefits, rather than its features, marketers change needs to wants. Changing a need to a want increases the probability of the sale and of customer satisfaction.

### What Is a Market?

A market is a group of people or organizations that need a product and have the ability, willingness, and authority to purchase the product. Authority to purchase the product means being socially and legally authorized to purchase. The group of people or organizations must want the product. It must satisfy a need. To satisfy this need, the customers must be willing to use their buying power – exchanging money, physical goods, or services for the product.

Markets are broadly placed in two categories: **consumer and business-to-business (B2B)**. These two markets vary quite a bit in their characteristics. Consumers buy to consume or benefit from their purchase in a personal way. B2B markets are sometimes called industrial markets and have four basic types:

o *Producer* markets are markets where individuals or businesses purchase products for use in producing other products.
o *Reseller* markets are intermediaries such as retailers or wholesalers that purchase finished products to resell at a profit.
o *Governmental* markets consist of federal, state, and local governments. Governments purchase products for their operations and to provide citizens with such things as roads, schools, national defense, and water.
o *Institutional* markets would include not-for-profit organizations, churches, hospitals, private schools, and charitable organizations.


**Target Markets**

A target market is a group of people or organizations to which a firm directs its marketing efforts. The group is specifically "targeted" as a purchaser for the firm's output. The firm's marketing efforts are tailored to meet the needs of the target market. The group of customers are similar or have certain similar characteristics or wants. The firm will maintain a marketing mix for each of its target markets.

Target markets are not limited to small markets. A target market can be quite large. A target market just needs to be somewhat homogeneous.

A marketing-oriented manager practices target marketing. This manager sees everyone as different, but with some similar characteristics.

The marketing strategy is adjusted to meet the needs of the target market.

### The Marketing Mix

The marketing mix is a combination of decisions relating to four main categories:

o **Product**
o **Price**
o **Promotion**
o **Distribution**

Managers develop a mix of product, price, promotion, and distribution that best addresses the needs of the target market, the goals and resources of the organization, and the number and competencies of competitors. The marketing mix is a dynamic, ever changing and adapting mix of product, price, promotion, and distribution. The marketing mix represents the *controllable variables* for the firm that it will use to appeal to its target market. The marketing mix variables can be thought of as **demand variables**, as these are the variables that the organization uses to manage demand.

### Mass Marketing

Mass marketing is a typical production-oriented approach to marketing that aims at "everyone" with the same marketing mix. Remember that mass marketing and mass marketers are not the same thing. Mass marketing is about trying to sell to everyone and mass marketers like Target and Wal-Mart are focusing on clearly defined target markets. These target markets may be large and spread out, but they are still clearly defined. Target and Wal-Mart are not trying to sell to "everyone."

A production-oriented manager sees everyone as basically similar, and practices mass marketing.

### Market Segmentation

Market segmentation is dividing a market into smaller, relatively similar groups. Both not-for-profit organizations and for-profit businesses use market segmentation for both consumer and business-to-business markets.

The common bases for market segmentation are as follows:

o **Geographic** segmentation divides markets based on their geographic location. The demand for some products will vary depending on geographic region. Using winter boots as an example, in Michigan, winter boots are a much-demanded item, but in Florida, winter boots are a specialty item. Another aspect of geographic segmentation is that population concentrates in urban areas; much of a country's population will be found on a small percentage of its land area.

o **Demographic** segmentation is the most common method of segmentation. It defines consumer groups based on such things as age, income, occupation, education, gender, and family life cycle.

o **Psychographic** segmentation increases a marketer's insight into consumer buying behavior. This type of segmentation divides a population into groups that have similar lifestyles, motives, values, personality attributes, and psychological characteristics.

o **Product-related** segmentation divides consumers into groups based on such things as the benefits that people seek when they buy a product, or the usage rates for a product.

### The Environmental Factors

Marketing managers must take into account various environmental factors when making target market and marketing mix decisions. The environmental factors can exert considerable influence on marketing management and marketing success. The environmental factors are as follows:

- o **Competitive** factors relate to what the firm's competitors are up to. For example, say that a competitor has just introduced its product in a large variety of colors when previously only three colors were standard in the industry. If customers like the color choice, then a firm may be forced to add additional colors to its product to stay competitive with its rival.
- o **Economic** factors are generally about the state of the economy. When the economy is strong, people have more money to spend and are more apt to spend it on premium-priced products. This is sometimes called a bullish market, or it is said that people are bullish about the economy. During weakened economic times, people have less money, are usually more pessimistic about economic matters, and are more conservative in their spending. This is sometimes called a bearish market.
- o **Political/Legal/Regulatory** factors concern governmental activities. For example, if the government requires certain emission standards for vehicles, then sellers must change their products to meet those new standards.
- o **Social/Cultural** factors have a strong impact on marketing. If a product becomes less accepted by our society or culture, then it will become much more difficult to sell. An example of this would be fur coats. In the 1950s, fur coats were a much desired product, with movie stars proudly wearing their furs in public. Today, a movie star that wears a fur coat would risk public disapproval and probably lost sales at the box office. Products that become more socially or culturally accepted are much easier to sell, and producers can look forward to industry sales growth.
- o **Technological** factors are commonplace today. Products that were once in high demand have lost consumer interest because of newer products with more advanced technology. A good example of this is VCRs. Once a highly sought after product that was cutting edge technology, VCRs are now passed over in favor of DVDs.

Changing environmental factors require marketing managers to make constant adjustments to their marketing mixes and target market strategies. The one certainty that marketing managers face is that there will be continuing change. For the well managed company, change is not bad - change is good – because change creates opportunity for the skilled and competent firm.

## Sales Forecasting

A key activity of marketing is the development of the sales forecast. A sales forecast is an estimate of sales for a particular time period. All areas of the firm will make decisions based on marketing's sales forecast. For example, operations will make its decisions on how much product to make based on expected sales, and finance will calculate needed capital based on these same expectations, not to mention marketing's decisions regarding product, price, promotion, and distribution. An accurate sales forecast will lead to better decisions by the firm's managers. If the sales forecast is found to be unacceptable, managers can then work on strategies to change the forecast. For example, if sales are forecast to decrease, marketing managers can work on product adjustments to make the product more attractive to customers, or increase promotion or distribution.

In making the sales forecast, it is important that the sales forecast is what is *expected* to happen and not what is hoped for. Expectation and hope are very different. Always make sure that sales forecasts are based on expectation. This is best accomplished by drilling down into the sales system: salesperson by salesperson, customer by customer, product by product, and month by month to determine what can be expected to happen in terms of sales.

Because of its vital importance, sales forecasting gets considerable attention in business. Sales forecasting is done in basically one of three ways:

- o **Time Series** methods are based on the idea that what has happened in the past will continue into the future. A simple example: if we have sold 1,000 pizzas per week in each of the past 6 weeks, then by time series thinking, we would forecast sales of 1,000 pizzas in the upcoming week.

- o **Causal methods** attempt to find a variable or variables that will help to predict future sales. An example is ice cream sales. As outside temperatures rise in the summer, ice cream sales have a tendency to go up. Customers are more interested in going out for an ice cream cone on a warm summer evening than they are on a snowy January day. We can then say that temperature is a variable that affects ice cream sales.
- o **Qualitative methods** are based on the judgment and experience of the forecaster.

Generally, time series and causal methods are the best choice for short-term sales forecasting. They are less expensive, faster, and more accurate in the short-term than qualitative methods. Qualitative methods are the favored method used in making long-term forecasts because they produce more accurate long-term forecasts.

Another important aspect of sales forecasting is the range, or deviation of error. A forecast with a small range or deviation of error is more favorable and reliable for decision-making. A sales forecast of 100,000 units with a lowest expected sales of 97,000 units and a highest expected sales level of 102,000 units, is one example. The range of 97,000 to 102,000 units is fairly small – a range most firms can handle. However, if the sales forecast has an expected high range of error or deviation, then the firm will struggle with making reliable and effective decisions. The uncertainty of what is to come is simply greater. More certainty is good for decision-making, and less certainty makes decision-making more difficult and less reliable.

### The Eight Universal Marketing Functions

Marketing has eight universal functions.
Exchange Functions:
1. **Buying** – Ensuring that product offerings are available in sufficient quantities to meet customer demands
2. **Selling** – Using advertising, personal selling, and sales promotion to match products to customer needs

Physical Distribution Functions

3. **Transporting** – Moving products from their place of production to locations that are convenient for purchasers

4. **Storing** – The warehousing of products until needed for sale

Facilitating Functions

5. **Standardizing and Grading** – Ensuring that product offerings meet quality and quantity controls of size, weight, and other variables

6. **Financing** – Providing credit to channel members, such as wholesalers and retailers and to consumers

7. **Risk Taking** – Dealing with uncertainty about future customer purchases

8. **Securing Marketing Information** – Collecting information about competitors, consumers, and channel members for use in making marketing decisions

## Global Marketing

There are several factors that have forced countries to extend their economic views to events outside their own borders. First, the growth of electronic commerce and similar computer technologies brings previously isolated countries into the buyer and seller marketplace regardless of their global location. Second, countries are attempting to increase international trade between nations. Third, is the reality of the interdependence of the world's economies, as no nation consumes all of its outputs or can produce all of the raw materials and finished goods desired by its citizens.

Evidence of this trend is the Euro as a common currency of European nations to facilitate trade. Another example is that approximately 80% of Coca-Cola's sales occur outside the United States.

For marketers, global marketing strategies can sometimes be very similar to national strategies. However, in many cases marketing strategies must be changed significantly to adapt to different cultural and legal requirements abroad, or to unique tastes of different cultures.

The soft drink 7-Up is a good example. In the United States the number "7" is considered by some people as good luck and therefore the name 7-Up makes a great name in our country. In China, however, the number "7" is considered by some to be unlucky, and who wants to buy a soft drink with an unlucky name?

## The Marketing Mix in More Detail

### PRODUCT

The first step in creating a marketing mix is to develop a product strategy. The other marketing mix variables – pricing, promotion, and distribution – must accommodate the chosen product strategy. Specifically, the product strategy is all about offering a product that is designed to satisfy customer needs. Offerings can be quite different and still satisfy the same need of customers.

Most sellers offer customers a series of related products called a **product line**. By creating complete product lines instead of just individual products, companies can benefit by increasing growth opportunities, improving the firm's position in the marketplace, making the best use of its resources, and using the product life cycle to its advantage.

The assortment of individual offerings and product lines that a firm offers is called its **product mix**. A good product mix will maximize a company's sales potential within the constraints of its resources. Therefore, effective management of the product mix is becoming more and more important as firms attempt to get the most from their resources.

The two critical components of product strategy are new product planning and introducing, building, and maintaining an identity for products through a concept called branding. **Branding** is about differentiating a firm's products from those of its competitors. A **brand** is a design, symbol, term, name, or a combination thereof that identifies the products of a company. For example, Coke can easily be identified by the shape of its bottle, its familiar color of red, or its distinctive lettering style for the name, "Coca-Cola." Good branding can result in **brand loyalty**, where customers recognize, prefer, and in the ultimate stage insist on a certain brand. Every marketer would love to be in the position where customers refuse to accept alternative products and instead search for the desired brand.

The value that branding can give a product in the marketplace is called **brand equity**. A strong brand can increase sales and provide the potential to receive premium prices. A good way to think about branding is that the brand is the company's promise(s) to the customer. A strong brand cannot be purchased with money. A strong brand must be earned by performance – the delivering of superior products to customers. The psychological service component of the bundle of physical goods and services introduced in the operations chapter is closely associated with branding. A company with a strong brand is a company that keeps its promises to its customers – the customer receives considerable psychological service when dealing with a seller that keeps its promises. Frequently, customers are more than willing to pay for this psychological service. Because of this, the best companies work hard at keeping their promises to customers and maintaining and building the brand.

Manufacturers can create brand loyalty not just with consumers, but with its other customers, such as retailers. This can be accomplished with retailers by such things as on-time delivery, quality, etc. - in other words, keeping its promises to the retailers. This type of brand loyalty is much less expensive to create than consumer brand loyalty through advertising. So if a company does not have the resources to create consumer brand loyalty, it can create retailer brand loyalty with far fewer resources by keeping its promises to the retailer. The retailer will then help it create consumer brand loyalty.

**Packaging** is another important part of product strategy and branding. Packaging protects the product from spoilage and damage. In addition, packaging can assist in the marketing of the product. Packaging must do all of this at a reasonable cost. We have all been influenced by packaging when making purchase decisions; we know that packaging can make a big impact on which products we choose to purchase.

A firm must develop and introduce new products as its offerings enter the maturity and decline stages of the product life cycle if it is to continue to prosper. The ability to develop and introduce new products successfully is a key factor in the long-term health of a firm. New products also create growth opportunities and a competitive advantage over rivals. Developing new products is expensive and risky. In addition, there is the increasing drive to introduce new products faster, without sacrificing quality.

One tool that is used in product strategy is called **value analysis**. Value is defined as the ratio of usefulness to cost. *Cost* measures the amount of resources that are used to produce the product and can be calculated exactly. *Usefulness* is a relative term; it describes the functionality or want satisfaction that the customer assigns to the product. A product's performance, features, and reliability can be used to describe usefulness. If a firm can figure out how to lower the cost while maintaining usefulness, then value will go up for the customer. Likewise, if cost can be held steady and usefulness increased by adding features, improved performance, or better reliability, then value will go up for the customer. The best of all worlds occurs when cost is decreased and usefulness is increased. All these scenarios are likely to increase sales or make the product easier to sell. This is the value ratio concept discussed in the operations chapter.

Consumer products typically have a product life cycle. The **product life cycle concept** describes the stages that a new product goes through from its beginning until its end. The product life cycle has four major stages:
- o Introduction
- o Growth
- o Maturity
- o Decline

The product life cycle is concerned with industry sales and industry profits of a product category or type, rather than sales and profits of individual brands.

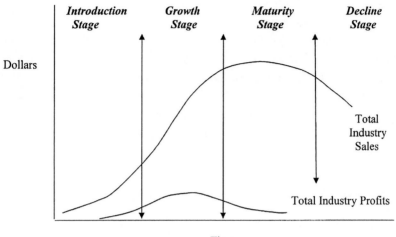

Some things to remember about the product life cycle:
o   Individual brands may not follow the industry life cycle pattern.
o   How broadly (or narrowly) a market is defined may change the life cycle stage.
o   Products increasingly have shorter and shorter life cycles – sellers would generally like to have longer life cycles.
o   Individual life cycle stages can vary in duration.

**The Introduction Stage**
Industry sales are low and unit prices are high as the new product is first introduced to the market.  Consumers are not aware of the product.  In this stage, marketing focuses on creating primary demand – creating awareness in the minds of consumers about the advantages and uses of the new product.

The operations function focuses its efforts on learning how to make the product, working out production problems, and solving product reliability issues.

### The Growth Stage

Consumers are aware of the product, its advantages, and its uses. Operations is learning how to make the product better and cheaper...and in higher volumes. As prices come down, more and more consumers buy the product. This results in an overall increase in industry sales. Industry profits peak and begin to decline during this stage. Marketers' focus their attention on creating selective demand. This means to get consumers to demand not just the product category, but to demand the marketers' particular brand.

Most competitors enter the market in the growth stage.

### The Maturity Stage

In the mature stage, industry sales peak and begin to decline. Unit prices continue to go down as the operations function continues to lower its production cost per-unit. Prices get low enough that anyone who wants the product usually has purchased it. There is intense price competition between individual sellers. Less efficient sellers (those with higher costs per unit) begin to drop out of the product category. The focus of operations is on lowering costs per unit.

Marketing begins to segment the market extensively. Marketers seek to serve each segmented market (target market) well by creating marketing mixes for each segment that emphasize product attributes such as quality, reliability, and service (product differentiation). Large promotional outlays are common.

### The Decline Stage

In the decline stage, new product category innovations or shifts in consumer preferences bring about an absolute decline in industry sales. Price competition is intense. Firms with strong brands and successful market segmentation strategies…and low costs…can still make money, but the end is in sight.

### Extending the Product Life Cycle
Marketers will attempt to extend product life cycles by:
- o   Finding new uses for the product
- o   Increasing the number of users of the product
- o   Increasing the frequency of use by current customers
- o   Changing package sizes or product quality

Most consumers have a sense that a product life cycle exists. When you see a new product that you like, but you don't like the price – what do you do? You usually wait because you have learned that prices usually decline on new products. Now with your understanding of the product life cycle concept – you know why prices decline and you can now predict price declines with much greater accuracy. In addition, you are in a much better position to determine when it is the best time for you to purchase in a product category.

### PRICE
Price is the exchange value of a product in the marketplace. Pricing is a difficult task and a dynamic one. Prices shift in response to many variables. Some variables are external to the business, such as competitors' pricing and changes in technology. Other variables, such as costs or inventory levels, are internal. Price can also convey an image. Examples are that higher than average prices may indicate higher quality in the buyer's mind, and lower than average prices may make the buyer think that the product is a good value, or in reverse, make the buyer believe that the product is of lower quality. Prices also have a huge impact on the firm's overall profitability and market share. The objective is always a justifiable or fair price that is profitable.

Some firms make a product that is in competition with other similar products. In this situation, a market price already exists for the firm's output. Customers will not pay more than the existing market price, and there is no reason to charge less. Therefore the firm just sells at the market price (control of costs is very important in this scenario). Some examples of these products are chewing gum and candy bars.

### Cost-Plus Pricing

Other sellers must set their own prices. If the company sets its prices too high, customers will not buy its output. If prices are set too low, then the seller's costs may not be covered. One way that a seller can price products is to mark up cost. This is called **cost-plus pricing**. Cost-plus pricing is a common method of pricing in business.

*Selling Price = Cost + (% Markup X Cost)*

For example, if a seller uses a markup of 50%, then the seller would add 50% to the costs of its products to arrive at the selling price. If the product costs are $1, then the selling price would be $1.50. With cost-plus pricing, there are two main questions. First, what cost should be used? In business, it is frequently very difficult to accurately determine product costs, particularly when the firm makes many different products. Second, what markup should be used? Too low of a markup will result in prices that do not allow for a business-sustaining profit, and too high of a markup may result in lower unit sales. So, while the concept of cost-plus pricing is simple enough, its application is far from easy.

### How the Economist Approaches Pricing

When a seller raises its prices, unit sales will usually fall. Pricing becomes a balancing act between the benefits of a higher price per unit and lower unit sales, or a lower price per unit and higher unit sales.

**Elasticity** is a measure of responsiveness of buyers and sellers to changes in price. The elasticity of demand is the percentage change in the quantity of a physical good or service demanded divided by the percentage change in its price. For example, if a price increase of 10% for milk results in a 5% reduction in the quantity of milk demanded, the elasticity of demand would be .5 (5 divided by 10). Amounts less than 1.0 are said to be inelastic. So in this example of milk, we would say that the demand for milk is inelastic. On the other hand, if a price increase of 10% for milk resulted in a 20% decrease in the quantity demanded, the elasticity of demand would be 2.0 (20 divided by 10). Amounts over 1.0 are said to be elastic.

It works the same way for supply. For example, if sellers will supply 15% more of a product if the price increases 5%, the elasticity of supply is elastic (15 divided by 5 is 3.0) because 3.0 is greater than 1.0. In reverse, if sellers supply 5% more of a product with a price change of 15% then the elasticity of supply for the product is inelastic (5 divided by 15 is .33 which is less than 1.0).

What all this means is that product with high elasticity of demand will have customers that are very sensitive to price changes. Low elasticity of demand means that customers are less sensitive to price changes. For sellers, high elasticity of supply indicates that sellers are sensitive to price changes and low elasticity of supply tells us that sellers are less sensitive to price changes.

What determines elasticity? First, the availability of substitutes or complements influence the elasticity of demand for a product. For example, if buyers have difficulty finding substitutes or complements, then the elasticity of demand would tend to be more inelastic. If many substitutes are available and are easily obtained, then the elasticity of demand would be elastic. Second, the percentage of a person's monthly expenditures spent on a product will affect elasticity. Higher percentages spent are generally more elastic than lower percentages spent. Third, elasticity depends on whether the product is a luxury or a necessity. Necessities usually are more inelastic and luxuries more elastic. Finally, demand frequently shows less elasticity in the short run than in the long run. The long run gives people time to adjust their needs and buying patterns, thus creating more elasticity. An example is gasoline. In the very near-term, increases in gas prices don't change demand all that much. But in the longer-term, if higher gas prices were to continue, people would start to lower their demand for gas by car-pooling, buying higher miles per gallon cars, riding bicycles, figuring out how to drive less, and so on.

### The Target Costing Approach
Target costing is a method where the seller determines the maximum allowable cost for a product and then develops a product that satisfies the customer, but can still be made within the maximum allowable cost.

*Target cost = Anticipated selling price – Desired profit*

Target costing works well because of two characteristics of markets and costs: first, many sellers do not have much control over prices that can be charged…supply and demand (the market) controls the price. Thus, the anticipated selling price is taken as a given in target costing (an uncontrollable variable). What is controllable, at least to some extent, is the product's cost. Second, the cost to produce a product is primarily determined in the design stage of a product. Once designed and in production, there is not much that can be done to significantly reduce cost. Therefore, the design stage is the key…and target costing emphasizes the importance of good design in product profitability.

### Other Pricing Methods
The number of pricing methods is endless. I have listed a few methods, just to get you started in thinking about pricing. Marketing courses cover this subject in great detail.

### Pricing in the 21st Century
With e-commerce, buyers can now compare prices quickly. This increases the already intense price competition. Consumers will reap the rewards of this competition. Sellers will be forced to become more efficient, as buyers can rapidly find the lowest prices. In the past, the buyer had no access to systems to quickly compare prices; this kept prices more static allowing firms to be less efficient than they could have been. Customers are now demanding (and receiving) lower prices, better quality, and better service. We can expect this trend to continue into the foreseeable future.

## PROMOTION

Promotion is the communication link between the seller and the buyer. **Promotion** seeks to inform, persuade, and influence buyers in their purchases. Promotion has five basic objectives:

o Provide information to consumers and others
o Differentiate a product from competitor's products
o Increase demand
o Stabilize sales
o Improve a product's value

To achieve organizational objectives and satisfy customers, a business must have the proper mix of promotion. A firm's **promotional mix** consists of five elements:

o **Advertising** is a paid, non-personal communication by various media such as TV, radio, newspapers, and magazines. Its purpose is to inform or persuade. Advantages: allows complete control over the final message; has a relatively low cost per exposure; reaches many potential customers; and can be adapted to targeted audiences or mass audiences. Disadvantages: results are difficult to measure; and it usually will not close sales.

o **Sales promotion** is a broad category that consists of marketing activities other than advertising, personal selling, direct marketing, and public relations. Examples of sales promotion include rebates, coupons, trade shows, displays, contests, samples, and product demonstrations. Sales promotion provides a short-term incentive for buyers, often in combination with other forms of promotion. Advantages: easy measurement of results; gets an immediate response from the buyer; creates product awareness; and generates short-term sales increases. Disadvantages: very difficult to differentiate from competitors' efforts; impersonal; and can be costly. The typical company spends as much as three times more on sales promotion than it does on advertising.

o **Personal selling** is the seller's promotional message presented person-to-person. Advantages: generates an immediate response from the buyer; the seller can tailor the message to the buyer and answer questions or solve complaints that the buyer may have; and effectiveness is measurable. Disadvantages: has a high cost per sales presentation; and relies heavily on the ability of the salesperson.

o **Public relations** are about a firm's communications with its various publics. The firm's publics include employees, suppliers, stockholders, the general public, and the government, as well as customers. Advantages: can create a positive attitude toward a product or a company; and can improve the credibility of a company or product. Disadvantages: difficult to accurately measure effect on sales; and typically involves considerable effort directed to non-marketing oriented objectives.

o **Direct marketing** includes the internet, telephone marketing, infomercials on TV, and direct mail. Advantages: generates an immediate response; produces measurable results; allows for customized messages; and covers a broad audience with a targeted message. Disadvantages: sometimes has a high cost per customer; customers frequently are annoyed (from telephone calls for example); sometimes creates an image problem; and mailings rely on an accurate and well-suited mailing list.

If people cost is a part of sales cost, the goal should be to reduce people cost in sales as a percentage of sales revenue. If selling is by the internet, then the goal should be to reduce internet costs as a percentage of sales revenue. The same would be true for advertising and sales promotion. Note that the goal is not to reduce the cost; the goal is to reduce the cost as a percentage of sales revenue. This means that the cost can stay the same – but if sales revenue increases, the percentage of the cost to sales revenue will go down. The sales cost can even go up – sales revenue just needs to be going up faster than the cost.

## DISTRIBUTION

Distribution moves goods and services from sellers to buyers. The two main parts of distribution are the distribution channel and logistics. Good distribution channels and effective logistics provide buyers with convenient ways (time, place, and possession utility) to obtain the goods and services that they desire. Customers generally have different needs with respect to time, place, and possession utility as they make different purchases. A "different purchase" could be different types of products or even be the same product, but the use of the product may be different. For example, milk purchased for daily nutritional needs would have a different distribution requirement than milk purchased on the morning of July 4th to make Fourth of July ice cream. Factors such as the weather, gas prices, and economic cycle can also impact the distribution needs of customers.

A **distribution channel** is an organized system of marketing entities that promotes the physical flow and ownership of products from the seller to the buyer. The choice of distribution channel should support the firm's overall marketing strategy.

**Logistics** is the process of coordinating the flow of goods, services, and information among members of the marketing channel. Good logistical systems support customer service.

A basic distribution decision that a firm must make is whether to do all the distribution itself (such as direct-to-customer e-commerce selling), or to use wholesalers, retailers, and other specialists. A firm may want to distribute directly to the final customer because it can control the entire marketing job. It may think that it can do the work of serving target market customers at a lower cost (efficiency), or do the work better (effectiveness). Doing a better job in this case may simply mean that the firm has a stronger focus on the particular product(s) or target market(s).

Obviously, the firm should seek out the most efficient (lowest cost) and most effective (the best job) distribution methods for its products.

The method of distribution will be influenced by the product life cycle. As products mature (lower margins, higher volumes), they typically need broader distribution to reach different target customers (extensive market segmentation). This means that a product can benefit from different distribution strategies during different product life cycle stages. What can make this difficult is that distribution strategies frequently are harder to change than product, price, or promotion strategies in both time and money. With this thought in mind, distribution strategies must be crafted with great care, and distribution decisions must be made considering their long-term effects.

### Distribution - The Ideal Market Exposure

Some product classes require much less market exposure than other product classes. The ideal market exposure makes a product available enough to satisfy target customers' needs, but availability (time, place, and possession utility) does not exceed the needs of the target customers. Excess market exposure only increases the total costs of marketing, resulting in a higher total delivered cost to the customer. There are three main categories of market exposure:

o **Intensive distribution** is the sale of the product through all suitable and responsible retailers who are willing to stock and sell the product. The product is essentially available "everywhere." Examples include Pepsi, Crest toothpaste, and Kraft cheese.

o With **selective distribution,** only wholesalers and retailers that will give the product special attention sell it. A good example is a clothing brand that is sold only in certain retail stores.

o **Exclusive distribution** allows the sale of the product by only one marketing intermediary in a particular geographic area. For example, new vehicles may only be sold in an authorized dealership. The number of dealerships and the location of the dealerships (as well as many other factors) are strictly controlled by the vehicle manufacturer.

## Marketing Chapter Conclusion

Marketing and selling are becoming more and more important. One reason is that many sellers have become very competent at operations...sellers from all around the globe. Since more sellers are producing excellent products than in the past, great marketing and selling are needed to effectively compete in a product area. Besides making great products, the operations of most companies can produce huge amounts of product...meaning if demand is present, more product can usually be produced in a short amount of time. In the longer term, more capacity can be built to make even more product if demand is present. What this means is that because operations has become so efficient, and as it continues to get more and more efficient...marketing and selling will see an increased emphasis.

The functions of operations and marketing can use large amounts of money. From where does this money come? It is time to turn our attention to the third functional area of a business – finance.

# CHAPTER 9

*Finance*

### What Is Financial Management?

Financial management includes everything that is involved in acquiring money and using it effectively. The primary goal of financial management in business is to maximize the value of owners' equity. With a corporation, this means maximizing the current value per share of the existing stock.

Good financial decisions increase the value of owners' equity, and poor decisions decrease it. This concept can also be used in not-for-profit organizations. The equivalent to maximizing the value of owners' equity for a not-for-profit organization is maximizing the benefits available to those served.

### Some Finance Basics

### Simple and Compound Interest

**Simple interest** means that once interest is earned, it is not reinvested. For example, if we had a savings account at a bank with a balance of $100 earning 4% interest, the interest per year would be $4. With a simple interest computation, we would withdraw the interest of

$4 from the account at the end of the year. The account balance would remain at $100, not growing because we are withdrawing the earnings (interest) from the account every year.

In contrast, **compound interest** means that the interest is reinvested. In our savings account example from above, we started with a balance of $100. Interest of $4 would be earned in year one. The interest would be left in the account in the case of compound interest, making the new balance $104 at the end of year one. The account would earn 4% on $104 in year two, or $4.16. The new balance at the beginning of year three would be $108.16. Interest at 4% would be earned on $108.16 in year three, totaling $4.33. The balance of the account at the beginning of year four would be $112.49.

### The Time Value of Money Concept

The time value of money concept is about the relationship between a dollar today and a dollar in the future. The concept of the time value of money has two components:

o **Future value** asks, if we do something today, what will we have in the future? Future value is something that is frequently asked by individuals. An example is, "If I invest $1,000 today, how much will my investment be worth in 10 years?" Or, "If I invest $3,000 per year in a retirement account earning a 7% rate of return, how much money will I have at retirement in 20 years?"

o **Present value** asks, if we receive something in the future, what is it worth today? Businesses frequently ask present value questions. For example, "What is the value today of $1,000 of net operating income received five years from now?"

Present and future value can be explained by using the example from the compound interest section. We started with $100 that earned 4% compound interest:

| | Present value | Future values ——————➤ | | |
|---|---|---|---|---|
| Balance | $100 | $104 | $108.16 | $112.49 |
| Years into the future | 0 | 1 | 2 | 3 |

The present value is $100 and the future values are $104, $108.16, and $112.49 in this example. We could continue to calculate future values for years 4, 5, 6, and so on.

### The Three Basic Questions of Business Financial Management

The business financial manager is primarily concerned with three basic questions:

**Question #1 – "In what area (or areas) of business do we want to be involved?"** Meaning, what long-term investments should be made? What types of buildings, machinery, equipment, and other assets will we need to pursue this line or lines of business?

The process of planning and managing a firm's long-term investments is called **capital budgeting**. In capital budgeting, the financial manager seeks to identify investment opportunities that are more valuable to the firm than their cost of acquisition. Effective capital budgeting requires the firm to estimate future cash flows from an investment. To estimate future cash flows, the manager must evaluate:
o The **size** of the future cash flows
o The **timing** (when received) of the future cash flows
o The **risk** of not receiving the future cash flows

Another way to look at capital budgeting is that the value of the cash flow generated by an asset should be worth more than the cost of the asset. An asset will usually produce inflows of cash (usually sales revenue) and outflows of cash (usually expenses) in any given time period.

*Inflows of Cash - Outflows of Cash = Net Cash Flow*

Once net cash flows are estimated, we must then account for varying sizes of net cash flows, when the net cash flows are received, and the risk of not receiving them.

We instinctively know that we would rather have a dollar today than a dollar one year from now for these reasons:

o Since the size of the cash flow (one dollar) is the same for either now or one year from now in this example, we would rather have the dollar now because of interest. Suppose we invest the dollar; one year from now we would have the dollar plus interest. If we spend the dollar, we would generally rather have the product today rather than one year from now. If we use the dollar to pay off a debt, then we would save the interest that we would have had to pay on the debt. Later is only better than now when we can see that we will receive more later than what we will receive now.

o Receiving the dollar today is certain, but receiving the dollar one year from now is less certain. Uncertainty is risk. The greater the uncertainty, the greater the risk. To willing assume risk, one must see that they have the potential to receive more in the future than now. If the amounts received both now and in the future are the same, it makes no sense to assume any risk – take the dollar now.

Managers typically account for size, timing, and risk by using present value analysis. **Present value** analysis converts future net cash flows into what they are worth today, or their present value. The process of calculating the present value of a future cash flow is called **discounting**. Discounting is the opposite of compounding. The discount rate is similar to an interest rate, except the firm is receiving rather than paying. For example, say we have a discount rate of 10% and will be receiving one dollar one year from now. We know that if we had the dollar today, we could invest it at 10% and have $1.10 one year from now. So what is a dollar received one year from now at a 10% discount rate worth today?

$$Present\ Value\ X\ 1.1\ =\ \$1$$
$$or$$
$$Present\ Value\ =\ \$1\ \div\ 1.1\ =\ \$.909$$

A dollar received one year from now at a 10% discount rate is worth 90.9 cents today. We could take $.909 and invest it at 10% and have $1 one year from now.

The farther into the future that a net cash flow is, the smaller its present value. For example, net cash flows received one year from now are worth much more to the firm than net cash flows received seven years into the future. By adding up all discounted cash flows for an asset, the manager calculates the **net present value (NPV)** of the asset. Positive net present value investments by the firm will increase the value of the firm. The greater the positive NPV, the more value is created. Negative net present value investments by the firm will decrease the value of the firm.

**Question #2 – "Do we bring in other owners (equity), or do we borrow the money (debt) to purchase assets?"** In other words, from where will the money come to pay for the investment in business assets? The advantage of debt is that owners do not have to give up any of their ownership in the firm. The disadvantage of debt is that it must be paid back with interest, usually on a predetermined payment schedule. Interest is simply the cost of using someone else's money. How much interest is paid is determined by how long the money is used, how much money is used, and how much risk the lender has in receiving its money back.

The advantage of bringing in other owners is that the firm is not legally obligated to pay back the new owners their investment, or to pay any accumulated interest or returns on that investment. The main disadvantage of equity financing is that the current owners' percentage share of the business will be reduced, or diluted.

A firm's **capital structure** is the specific mixture of long-term debt and equity that the firm uses to finance its operations. The mixture chosen will affect both the risk and the value of the firm. Increased debt increases the risk for the firm, as it must legally pay interest and borrowed amounts to lenders. Increased equity will decrease the firm's risk, as no payments are required to be made to owners. So the questions are:

- o What mixture of debt and equity is best for the firm?
- o What are the least expensive sources of funds for the firm?
- o Exactly how and where should we raise the money? Examples of questions that may be asked are: "What types of equity and debt should be used, what are the expenses of long term financing, which lender should be used, or which loan type should we use?"

If risk is reduced by lower debt amounts, why do organizations borrow money? To understand why, we must first consider the order of who gets paid. Creditors (lenders) always have first claim on the assets of an organization. The owners receive only what is left after all the firm's creditors have been paid. Since the owners are paid last, the owners have the highest risk. The assumption of higher risk means that, on average and over time, the owners must receive a higher return than creditors. Creditors can accept a lower return (interest rate) because they are paid first. This means that debt financing is generally less expensive than equity financing.

Another reason that a business may choose debt over equity is that the current owners do not want to give up their current percentage of ownership. Additional equity reduces the current owners' share of the company. It could also be true that no new equity holders are currently available to the firm for a myriad of reasons.

So if debt is usually less expensive than equity, why don't firms borrow all the money they need and have no equity in the business at all? As debt increases, so does the risk of repayment for creditors. Increasing repayment risk will cause lenders to charge ever-increasing interest rates, eventually canceling out any cost advantage. The objective is to create the most favorable ratio, or mix, of debt and equity. Some of the considerations for this mix are:

- o Lowest average **cost of capital** (or financing), which can be calculated by using a weighted average for each category of financing. Certain mixes will produce lower costs of capital. A firm with a lower cost of capital than its competitors has an absolute financial advantage over those competitors. The **cost of capital** is the average rate of return the firm must pay to its long-term creditors and to stockholders for the use of their funds.
- o Needs, wants, and desires of the owners. Owners vary in the willingness to assume risk. Some people would rather have a smaller piece of the pie with less risk. Others would prefer to assume maximum risk to have the whole pie.
- o Particular financial needs of the business or the industry. Some businesses are in industries that have large variances in sales and net income. A firm facing such uncertainty must offset this business variability by lowering its financing risks. In this case, the firm would choose to have higher equity and lower debt. On the other side, a business with a very steady and reliable cash flow can more readily take on the extra risk of more debt.
- o Availability of debt financing and equity financing in the current marketplace. The marketplace is constantly changing, and sometimes debt is easier to obtain than other times. The same is true for equity financing. Another related item is the firm's credit rating. If the firm has a strong credit rating, credit will be more available and at a lower cost (interest rate).
- o Availability of security for debt. A secured loan is a loan that is backed by an asset or assets of the borrower. If the borrower is unable to repay the loan, the lender can seize the asset(s), sell it, and use the proceeds to repay the loan balance and interest due. An unsecured loan is one where the lender has no security. Secured loans are less risky than unsecured loans for lenders and therefore generally have a lower interest rate. The availability of security is always a key issue in receiving loans from lenders.

**Question #3 – "How will everyday financial activities be managed?"** This category refers to the receipt and disbursement of cash, such as collecting money from customers (sales revenue) and paying suppliers (cost of goods sold). **Working capital** refers to a firm's current assets and current liabilities. Net working capital is current assets less current liabilities. The process of managing working capital is called working capital management. Managing the firm's working capital is a day-to-day activity to ensure that the firm has sufficient cash and resources to continue its operations without costly interruptions. Some of the important questions are:

o Should we sell to customers on credit? If we do, what will be our credit policies and terms?

o How much cash should we keep on hand?

o How much inventory should we keep on hand? The amount of inventory will affect our *service level* to customers as discussed in the operations section.

o How will we obtain needed short-term financing? Should we purchase on credit, or borrow in the short-term and pay cash? If we do borrow in the short-term, how and where should we do it?

### Sources of Funds

An organization has four sources of funds:

o **Sales revenue** resulting in **net income** is the preferred method of increasing funds. It requires neither repayment as with debt or dilution of owners' equity. In other words, a profitable organization feeds itself. It becomes self-sustaining. A disadvantage of extra debt or equity is that it is sometimes wasted. First, the debt or equity usually must be spent fast – because it has a cost of capital and needs a return – fast spending can result in wasted spending. Second, the quality of growth must be good, and the organization's competencies must grow – sometimes this is difficult to do quickly.

o **Debt capital** refers to borrowing money that must be repaid with interest.

- o **Equity capital** refers to increasing the amount of equity; this dilutes the percentage ownership of the current stockholders.
- o **Sale of assets** can also be a source of funds. If the assets sold are not productive for the firm, then such a sale is a good idea. However, the sale of productive assets can be very damaging to the firm and can even impact the effectiveness and efficiency of the firm. This weakening can result in lower sales revenue and net income, which in turn could lead to the need to sell more assets.

## Financial Planning

A financial plan specifies how financial goals will be achieved. Thus, the financial plan is a statement of what is to be done in the future. An appropriate goal for financial planning is to increase the value of owners' equity of the firm.

We can think of financial planning as short-run and long-run. Short-run planning is usually for a period within the next 12 months. Long-run planning generally means making decisions for two to five years into the future. This is called the planning horizon and is the first dimension of the planning process that must be established.

The second dimension of the planning process is called aggregation. Aggregation means that all of the firm's investment proposals and activities are added up to create one aggregate amount.

Finally, the financial manager uses **scenario analysis** (described in Chapter 3). Based on alternative sets of assumptions, the manager calculates the worst case scenario, the probable case scenario, and the best case scenario, as well as other possible scenarios. Scenario analysis forces managers to carefully think through all assumptions and the range of probable outcomes. Another benefit of scenario analysis is discovering the variables that are most sensitive to change. This is called **sensitivity analysis** (described in Chapter 3). For example, if we know that direct labor is a very sensitive variable in our success or failure, then we know we need to manage this variable with extra care and thoughtfulness.

### What Can Financial Planning Accomplish?

o **Explore Options** - the firm can create, analyze, and compare many different scenarios in a consistent and disciplined way. Scenarios can be fine-tuned for optimal effectiveness.

o **Examine the Interactions** - between new investments and operating activities and the methods of financing.

o **Avoid Surprises** - as Mark Twain once said, "Prediction is very difficult, particularly when it concerns the future." An objective of financial planning is to develop contingency plans – plans for what we will do if things turn out very different than expected, and to help to avoid surprises.

o **Ensure Feasibility and Internal Consistency** – the financial planning process forces managers to link all the goals and activities of the firm into an integrated unit. Managers must think about goals and establish priorities for the firm.

### The Ingredients of a Financial Planning Model

o The **Sales forecast** is the key element of financial planning. Sales forecasts are typically provided by the marketing function.

o **Pro forma statements** in the financial plan include a forecasted balance sheet, income statement, and statement of cash flows. These forecasted statements are called pro forma statements, or pro formas for short.

o **Asset requirements** in the plan should describe projected capital spending.

o **Financial requirements** in the plan should contain a section on the needed financing arrangements.

o The **Financial plug** is the designated source or sources of external financing needed to deal with any shortfall or surplus in financing.

o **Economic assumptions** made by the plan should be stated clearly.

## Sources of Debt and Equity Financing

The sources of debt and equity financing are short-term debt, long-term debt, and equity.

### Sources of Short-Term Debt Financing

Short-term financing is money repaid in one year or less. It is usually easier to obtain than long-term financing because the shorter repayment period means less risk for the lender, the total loan amounts in dollars are usually less, and there is usually a close working relationship between lender and borrower. The following are some examples of short-term debt financing:

- o **Bank loans** can be either secured or unsecured. In some cases, a business may arrange for a *line of credit*, which is a prearranged short-term loan.
- o **Commercial paper** is a short-term promissory note issued by a large corporation. No security is involved with commercial paper. The rate paid by the large corporation is usually slightly below the interest rate charged by banks for short-term loans. The ability to issue commercial paper is closely tied to the corporation's credit rating and its ability to repay the loan. A large corporation with an excellent credit rating and superior operating performance can raise large sums of money quickly via commercial paper.
- o **Trade credit** is business-to-business credit. Credit is extended by one business acting as the seller to another business acting as the buyer as an incentive for the buyer to purchase from the seller. In fact, 80 to 90 percent of all transactions between businesses involve some trade credit, making it the most used form of short-term debt financing. For some businesses, trade credit is the primary form of financing and the key to being in business. This is particularly true of many small businesses.
- o **Promissory notes to suppliers** are promissory notes written as a pledge by a borrower to pay a certain sum of money to a creditor by a specified date. Suppliers uncomfortable with extending trade credit may be willing to extend credit using

this method. The typical repayment period is 60 to 180 days. The borrower is obligated to pay interest in most cases.

o **Loans secured by inventory** have a promissory note, and the borrower must pay interest.

o **Loans secured by accounts receivable** have a promissory note, and the borrower must pay interest. A lender may lend up to 70 to 80 percent of the dollar amount of the receivables. The percentage loaned will depend on the quality of the receivable (risk of repayment) and the credit rating of the borrower.

Short-term creditors (suppliers for example) want to be paid on time and with no problems. In making credit decisions, these creditors focus on the borrower's primary sources of cash in the short run: cash flows and working capital. Some of the tools that are used to make the credit decision are:

o **Current ratio = Current assets ÷ Current liabilities**. The general rule of thumb for a favorable current ratio is 2.0 or greater. The current ratio is a useful tool, but is tricky to interpret. It is important to carefully look at the individual assets and liabilities involved before coming to any conclusions. For example, from a current ratio and short-term creditor perspective, a business with a greater proportion of cash and accounts receivable and a lesser proportion of inventory in its current assets would be a better risk than a company with most of its current assets tied up in inventory.

o **Acid-test ratio = (Cash + Account receivables) ÷ Current liabilities**. (Also called the quick ratio). The acid-test ratio is a tougher test than the current ratio, since inventory is removed from the current asset calculation. The idea with the acid-test ratio is to have only the more liquid (or "quick") current assets divided by current liabilities. An acid-test ratio of 1.0 or greater is preferred, but ratios as low as .3 are common. Like the current ratio, the acid-test ratio should be studied carefully, by looking at the individual assets and liabilities that make up the ratio.

o **Net working capital**. This is the excess of current assets over current liabilities. While plenty of net working capital makes short-term creditors more comfortable, it comes with a cost. The net working capital must be financed by either long-term debt or equity, both of which are expensive. For this reason, managers often want to minimize net working capital.

o **Accounts receivable turnover = Sales on account ÷ Average accounts receivable balance**. This is a measure of how fast credit sales are converted into cash. Obviously, collecting accounts receivables faster is better than collecting more slowly. The turnover figure can be used to calculate the **Average collection period = 365 days ÷ Accounts receivable turnover**. This gives us the average number of days it takes to collect a credit sale.

o **Inventory turnover = Cost of goods sold ÷ Average inventory balance.** This tells us how many times a firm's inventory has been sold and replaced during the year. Inventory turnover will vary from industry to industry, but generally a faster inventory turnover is desired. A company with a fast inventory turnover will have a lower average inventory balance (in relation to sales).

### Sources of Long-Term Debt Financing

The primary methods of long-term debt financing are long-term loans and corporate bonds.

o **Long-term loans** are typically repaid in three to seven years. Sources for long-term loans are commercial banks, insurance companies, pension funds, and in some cases manufacturers or suppliers in order to facilitate a sale.

o **Corporate bonds** are bonds issued by large corporations. The bonds are the corporation's written pledge that it will pay a specified amount of money (the face value of the bond) with interest. The corporation usually pays the bondholder interest every six months until the maturity date of the bond, when the corporation will pay the bondholder the face value of the bond. Corporations can raise huge amounts of money by selling bonds. Maturity dates for most corporate bonds range from 10 to 30 years.

Long-term creditors are interested in the firm's ability to repay its debts over extended periods of time. A tool that long-term creditors use to increase the probability of repayment is a set of loan covenants. These are restrictive covenants (or rules) in the loan agreement that require the borrower to do certain things, such as maintain certain levels of financial ratios, not pay dividends to stockholders, or sustain minimum levels of growth. Ultimately, the company must generate sufficient earnings to make scheduled payments to long-term creditors. Some of the other tools used by long-term creditors are:

o **Debt to equity ratio = Total liabilities ÷ Owners' equity**. This ratio shows the proportions of debt and equity that are being used to finance the firm's operations. Creditors like to see less debt and more equity, as this relationship reduces the lender's risk. In business, ratios of 0.0 (or no debt) to 3.0 (3 times more debt than equity) are common. Acceptable debt to equity ratios will vary from industry to industry. For example, industries with stable earnings can stand to carry more debt than industries with less stable earnings.

o **Interest coverage = Earnings before interest expense and income taxes ÷ Interest expense**. From the perspective of providing protection to long-term creditors, this is probably the most frequently used measure. Earnings before interest expense and income taxes represent the earnings that are available to make interest payments. A ratio of less than 1.0 would mean that the business does not have sufficient earnings to make its interest payments. A ratio of 2.0 or more may be considered sufficient by long-term creditors; what is considered adequate will vary from industry to industry and company to company.

**Sources of Equity Financing**

For our purposes of introduction to business, we will focus on three sources of equity financing: initial equity investment; additional equity investments; and retained earnings.

o An **initial equity investment** is usually required to start a business. If the business is formed as a corporation, that investment will be stock. If the business is a limited liability company, then the investment will be a membership.

o **Additional equity investments** may be made after the business starts to fund any activity that requires long-term financing, such as growth and expansion of capacity. The original owners may make this investment, new investors may be added, or a combination of current and new investors may provide the needed funding.

o **Retained earnings** is the after tax income (cash flow) of the company that is not distributed to the owners. A business may choose to retain all of its earnings to use as long-term financing.

The common stockholder typically focuses on stockholders' equity, dividends, and net income. An investor purchases common stock with the goal of receiving a return, either in the form of dividends received or in the form of an increase in the value of the common stock. The following are some of the tools used:

o **Earnings per share = Net income less preferred dividends ÷ Average number of common shares outstanding**. Net income less preferred dividends is the net income available to the common shareholders. This is probably the most widely used statistic used by investors, and the most reported by the media.

o **Price earnings ratio = Market price per share ÷ Earnings per share**. (Also called the PE ratio.) The PE ratio tells us that a stock is selling a certain number of times more than its current earnings per share. The PE ratio is a widely used ratio by investors. For example, if a stock has a high PE ratio, this usually means that investors think that the company has a strong potential for future earnings growth. Companies with lower perceived future earnings potential will sell at lower PE ratios.

o **Dividend payout ratio = Dividends per share ÷ Earnings per share**. This ratio gives us the portion of current earnings that are being paid out as dividends.

o **Return on total assets = Net income + [Interest expense X (1 – Tax rate)] ÷ Average total assets**. This is figuring return on assets a bit differently than we do as business managers. Investors like to add back interest to see what the company's earnings would have been if it had no debt. This allows investors to compare the ROAs of different companies with varying amounts of debt.

o **Financial Leverage.** This is the difference in the rate of return that the firm earns on its assets and the rate that the company must pay its creditors. Financial leverage is positive if the company's return on its assets exceeds the rate it pays its creditors. If the firm's return on its assets is less than the rate it pays its creditors, then financial leverage is negative. Positive financial leverage increases the wealth of the common shareholder and negative financial leverage reduces shareholder wealth.

## How Lenders Make Credit Decisions

Lenders are in the business of lending money, collecting the money at a later date with interest, and then lending the money out again. The lender's greatest fear is not receiving loan repayment with interest. It takes a lot of interest from other loans to recover lost principle (the loan amount) and interest from just one bad loan. For this reason, business lenders work hard to make only loans that they believe have a very strong chance of being repaid with interest and no hassles.

A primary tool used by lenders is called the **Five C's of Credit Management**. Most lenders build their credit policies around the Five C's. The Five C's are as follows:

o **Character** refers to the borrower's attitude toward credit obligations. Experienced lenders know that the borrower's attitude is a critical component of being repaid. The main tool that lenders use is the credit report. The credit report contains a summary of the firm's credit history, as well as other pertinent information, such as tax liens and legal judgments. Lenders want to see a history of on-time payments, no hassles, thoughtful use of credit, and no legal or tax problems.

- o **Capacity** is the firm's financial ability to meet its financial obligations. Lenders like to see profitable companies. Lenders will use ratios to determine a firm's capacity, such as return on assets, return on sales (margin), return on owners' equity, the current ratio, the acid-test ratio, accounts receivable turnover, inventory turnover (also called inventory velocity), and asset velocity.

- o **Capital** as used in the Five C's refers to the firm's net worth, which is defined as assets minus liabilities. Assets will usually be valued at fair market value and liabilities at the current loan balance. Interest due in the future is not included. The debt to equity ratio is used here. In general, the greater the firm's equity as compared to debt, the greater the chance that the lender will be repaid. Thus lenders prefer companies with more equity than debt. Lenders will look at the type of debt a business has. The type of assets that the firm owns and the quality of those assets will be of particular concern.

- o **Collateral (or security)** is an asset that the firm can pledge to the lender as security for the loan. If the borrower does not repay the loan or live up to any of the other loan agreements, then the lender can repossess the collateral and sell it to pay off the loan. Collateral reduces the risk for lenders; therefore, lenders like collateral and will offer lower interest rates for secured loans than for unsecured loans. Another tool used in this category by lenders is the loan to value ratio. The lender will divide the loan amount by the fair market value of the collateral to arrive at this ratio. A low loan to value ratio reduces the risk to the lender, meaning the value of the collateral is high in comparison to the loan amount.

- o **Conditions** refer to the general economic conditions that can affect a firm's ability to repay a loan. Other factors in this category are a firm's general economic strength, its relative strength within its industry, the type of product it sells, and its earnings potential.

## Historical Returns of Various Investments

To better understand finance, it is important to have a sense of what various types of investments have returned in the past and why the returns vary between investment categories. Let's start with the average annual returns for selected investment categories, and then I will explain why the returns are different in the next section of this chapter.

The average annual returns (1) for various investments from 1926 to 2003 were as follows:

| Investment | Average Return | Risk Premium |
|---|---|---|
| Inflation | 3.1% | |
| U.S. Treasury Bills | 3.8 | 0.0% |
| Long-term government bonds | 5.8 | 2.0 |
| Long-term corporate bonds | 6.2 | 2.4 |
| Large-company stocks | 12.4 | 8.6 |
| Small-company stocks | 17.5 | 13.7 |

Investment Definitions:
1. U.S. Treasury Bills (T-bills) with a three month maturity are the standard in defining the risk free-rate of return.
2. Long-term U.S. government bonds are bonds with a 20 year maturity.
3. Long-term corporate bonds are high-quality bonds with a 20 year maturity.
4. Large-company stocks are based on the Standard and Poor's (S&P) 500 index, which contains 500 of the largest companies (in terms of total market value of outstanding stock) in the United States.
5. Small-company stocks are composed of the stock corresponding to the smallest 20% of the companies listed on the New York Stock Exchange, again as measured by the market value of the outstanding stock.

**Average return** refers to the average return of the investment category from 1926 to 2003.

**Risk premium** is the amount of the return attributable to risk – the amount of the return over the risk free return (U.S. Treasury Bills). T-bills represent the risk-free rate, and thus have a risk premium of 0.0%.

(1) Source for the historical returns: "Fundamentals of Corporate Finance" 7th Edition by Stephen Ross, Randolph Westerfield, and Bradford Jordan (2006) McGraw-Hill Irwin

### Historical Returns and Frequency Distributions Or "Why Are the Rates of Return Different?"

OK, so what is risk premium? Why do stocks have a higher rate of return than bonds? Why do small-company stocks have a higher rate of return than large-company stocks?

As risk goes up, the average return on an investment will go up. Since T-bills represent the risk-free rate, they have a risk premium of 0.0%. Risk is essentially a measure of uncertainty or variability of the potential outcome (the return). Thus, the higher the risk premium, the greater the uncertainty of the return for any given year, and the greater the possible variability of the return in a given year.

For example, large-company stocks had their highest rate of return in 1933 at 52.95% and their lowest rate of return at negative 43.6% in 1931. That is a pretty wide range of potential outcomes. A more recent example is that investors lost 22.1% of their money in 2002 (a negative return of 22.1%), but had a positive return of 28.69 % over the very next year – 2003. To assume such uncertainty (risk), investors must receive higher average returns over time than less risky investments.

Next, we need to consider the difference between debt investments (bonds) and equity investments (stocks). With bonds, the borrower has a legal contract to pay the bond holder interest at a stated interest rate (stated on the bond), and to pay the face value of the bond on maturity. The payment of this contractual debt must occur before stockholders are paid. In other words, the stockholders get whatever is left after all the liabilities of the company are paid. Since the stockholders are the last to be paid and do not know how much they will be paid they have the greatest risk. Without higher average rates of return on equities (stocks), no one would invest in equities. In contrast, bond holders know how much they will be paid – interest at the stated interest rate on the bond, and the face value of the bond at maturity.

So why do long-term corporate bonds have a slightly higher average return compared to long-term U.S. government bonds? The reason is that long-term corporate bonds have a greater risk of default – non-payment of interest and the bond face value at maturity. The U.S. government bonds are a "safer" or "more certain" investment.

Small-company stocks have a higher average rate of return over large-company stocks because they have a greater variability in rate of return in any given year. Large-company stocks are more consistent, more predictable. When something is more predictable, it is less risky.

## Conclusion

We have made the product in the operations chapter (created supply), then learned about creating demand and selling the product in the marketing chapter, and finally, in the finance chapter, I have covered how money is acquired and allocated internally by a company. That leaves us with just three chapters, and your business framework will be ready to serve you.

## Exhibit 9-1: The Present Value of a Single Sum Table

I discussed the concepts of present value and future value earlier in the chapter. In this exhibit, I want to discuss present value in more detail. Let's start by looking at the present value of $1 to be received after various numbers of years.

| Number of Years | Interest Rate | | | |
| --- | --- | --- | --- | --- |
| | 5% | 10% | 15% | 20% |
| 1 | .9524 | .9091 | .8696 | .8333 |
| 2 | .9070 | .8264 | .7561 | .6944 |
| 3 | .8638 | .7513 | .6575 | .5787 |
| 4 | .8227 | .6830 | .5718 | .4823 |
| 5 | .7835 | .6209 | .4972 | .4019 |
| 6 | .7462 | .5645 | .4323 | .3349 |
| 7 | .7107 | .5132 | .3759 | .2791 |
| 8 | .6768 | .4665 | .3269 | .2326 |
| 9 | .6446 | .4241 | .2843 | .1938 |
| 10 | .6139 | .3855 | .2472 | .1615 |
| 20 | .3769 | .1486 | .0611 | .0261 |
| 30 | .2314 | .0573 | .0151 | .0042 |
| 40 | .1420 | .0221 | .0037 | .0007 |
| 50 | .0872 | .0085 | .0009 | .0001 |

The factor in the chart at a certain interest rate and number of years represents the present value of the $1 if it was received today, rather than in the future - hence, the term "present value."

Let's say that $1 will be received in 10 years at a 5% interest rate. Go to the 10 year row in the "number of years" column and then the

"5%" column. The factor is .6139. This means that $1 received 10 years from now at a 5% interest rate is worth 61.39 cents today ($1 times .6139).

What is $1 received 10 years from now at a 20% interest rate worth today? Go to the 10 year row in the "year" column again and then across to the "20%" column. The factor is .1615, or $1 received 10 years from now at a 20% interest rate is worth 16.15 cents today ($1 times .1615).

Note that in these examples, $1's present value is much less at a 20% interest rate than a 5% interest rate. This highlights two important points about present value:

1. As we go farther into the future (the number of years), the present value of the $1 becomes smaller and smaller. Observe this in the table…see how the factors get smaller and smaller as you go down a column.
2. As the interest rate increases, the present value of $1 will be smaller and smaller. Again, observe this in the table…as you move across a row, see how the factors get smaller and smaller.

What this all means is that when receiving something in the future, its present value will be based on two things: how long before we receive it, and what interest rate is used.

# CHAPTER 10

*Human Resources*

We looked at the employees of an organization from the perspective of the people side of a business to some degree in Chapter 6. Now, we need to look into this area in a bit more detail.

> There is an old joke that goes like this:
> *The organization of the future will
> be so technologically advanced that it
> will be operated by just one person and
> a dog. The person will be there to feed
> the dog, and the dog will be there to
> make sure that the person doesn't touch
> anything. (source: unknown)*

Many people have feared (and still do) that machines may someday eliminate the need for people in the workplace. What has happened is just the opposite; people are more important in organizations today than ever before. Yes, it is true that jobs are different...jobs are different and more important...and the jobs require more education and training than ever before in history.

The term "**human resources**," or simply "**HR**," implies that people have talents and skills that drive organizational performance. Successful organizations are very adept at bringing together many different types of people to achieve a common purpose…this is what human resources management is all about.

We must understand human behavior to work with people effectively. And, we need to be knowledgeable about the various systems and practices available to us to help us build a motivated and skilled workforce. At the same time, we have to consider legal, technological, economic, and social issues that either constrain or facilitate our efforts to achieve business goals.

### Creating a Competitive Advantage through the People in the Organization

Increasingly, organizations compete by establishing a set of core competencies (the operations objective that the firm wants to do better than its competitors – from the operations objectives in Chapter 7). Core competencies are integrated knowledge sets within an organization that deliver value to customers and differentiate it from competitors. These knowledge sets are imbedded in the members of the organization.

People are a source of competitive advantage when:
o They improve the effectiveness (provide something of value to customers) or efficiency (find ways to lower costs) of the company.
o Their contributions and capabilities are difficult to imitate. If competitors are unable to copy these contributions and capabilities, then competitive advantage is obtained.
o Their talents, skills, and knowledge are rare and therefore not equally available to competitors.
o These talents, skills, knowledge, and efforts must be synchronized and directed toward a clear set of priorities.

### Today's Model Employee Profile

The best companies today have a "model employee profile." These companies will interview many people to find folks with certain characteristics. Read some company advertisements relating to hiring and you will see the company's employee profile. An example of an advertisement by a large and very successful manufacturing company that I saw recently is as follows:

"Perspective applicants should:
o   Be committed to working in a fast-paced environment
o   Be flexible and open-minded
o   Have the ambition to succeed and build products that exceed customers' expectations
o   Be motivated to actively seek new challenges
o   Be committed to safety and quality
o   Be committed to open communication and teamwork"

This advertisement provides a good example of what employers are looking for these days. The employers are simply responding to the needs of the marketplace – what the consumer wants. The employer in this example has learned that the people in the company need the above characteristics if the company is going to be able to satisfy and retain customers. Note that there is no mention of past manufacturing experience. The focus is on things like flexibility and open-mindedness, exceeding customers' expectations, seeking new challenges, safety and quality, and communication/teamwork. Interesting stuff I think – an indication of the desired job skills in the early 21$^{st}$ century.

Since the environment in which the business operates changes regularly, it is important that people get used to the fact that the business changes frequently. Change is required to continue to satisfy and retain customers and make money. This means that the model employee profile changes and individual jobs change. Each of us, as individuals, needs to be able to develop new job skills over time – to be able to switch from an old job to a new job if necessary – hence, the request in the above job advertisement for people that are flexible and open-minded.

It is important to have a stable workforce to get good productivity from employees, to be able to continuously improve the company, and to retain good employees. But you don't want things to become stagnant or non-changing. This would indicate that the company probably has an obsolete business model, has the wrong people (maybe the right people for the past, but not for today and the future), or has the wrong jobs for today's needs.

Finally, a curious thing about people is that they are the only business resources that can leave an organization at will. A business asset such as a computer cannot just leave a business. But people can; they can just walk out the door and leave a business permanently.

## The Human Resources Manager

We have looked at the employee side of HR; now let's look at HR from the perspective of the HR Manager. I will start first with the competencies of the HR manager.

The required competencies of HR managers can be summarized as follows:
o HR professionals must know the business of their organization well.
o HR professionals are the organization's behavioral science experts.
o HR professionals must be able to manage change so that the HR activities are merged with the business needs of the organization.
o HR professionals must develop both trust and credibility with both internal and external customers.

Next let's look at who is responsible for human resources management. The responsibility for HRM is shared between line managers and HRM specialists. The following is a general outline of a typical organization:

**Line managers** are responsible for:
o Providing input into planning and job analysis

o Making the actual hiring decisions
o Recommending pay increases and promotions
o Completing performance appraisals of employees

The **HRM staff** is responsible for:
o Planning and job analysis
o Recruiting and selection
o Designing new employee orientation programs
o Developing and administering compensation systems and benefits packages
o Designing the performance appraisal system (generally)

**Line managers and the HRM staff** share the responsibility for:
o Delivering new employee orientation programs
o Training and development activities

## Compensation Systems

I have been talking about compensation systems, so now is good time to briefly cover these systems.

### Effective Employee Reward Systems
Effective employee reward systems generally consist of the following:
o The **compensation system** should:
  o Enable employees to satisfy their basic needs
  o Provide rewards comparable to those offered by other firms
  o Be distributed fairly within the organization

o **Employee benefits**:
  o Should recognize that different people have different needs, usually accomplished by offering a number or a variety of benefits (for example, different types of health insurance plans).
  o Employee benefits average about 28% of the cost of wages or salaries. This percentage will vary from company to

company. This means that for every $100 that is paid to an employee in either wages or salary, there is a 28% benefits cost on average or $28 in this example. The firm's cost is not $100; it is actually $128. If an employee has a salary of $40,000 per year, the company's actual cost is $40,000 plus 28% or $51,200.

### The Compensation System

The policies and strategies that determine employee compensation should provide for the employee's needs, while keeping people costs within reasonable limits. This is accomplished by making three separate management decisions:

- o The wage level should be relative to that of comparable firms.
- o The *wage structure* determines pay levels for all the positions within the firm.
- o Individual wages are the specific payments that individual employees receive.

### A Big Picture Look at Human Resources

Now for a big picture look at human resources.

### Human Resources and Horizontal Value Creation

Creating value horizontally as compared to creating value vertically requires a totally different set of skills. The shift is from command and control (vertical) to collaboration (horizontal), which we will cover in more detail in the Information Systems and the Flat-World chapter (Chapter 11), and in the Today's Business chapter (Chapter 12). What was needed and has happened is that a large group of managers, business consultants, information technology specialists, CEO's, employees, innovators, and business schools have gotten comfortable with and developed the skills and habits necessary to create value-adding processes using collaboration. Another way to look at this is that new business practices where needed, which were less about command and control and more about connecting and collaborating horizontally.

A company can now look at its employees as a pool of individual specialists. Individual specialists can be assembled into any number of collaborative teams. The team needed would depend on the requirements of the project. This means determining the desired outcomes first...then assembling a collaborative team that can get the job done.

### New People in the Global Economy

During the 1990s, approximately three billion people from China, India, Russia, Eastern Europe, Central Asia, and Latin America were increasingly allowed the opportunity to compete, collaborate, and participate in the global economy. Prior to that, they had lived in primarily closed economies with very vertical, hierarchical political and economic structures. In addition, India, China, and Russia all have a very high ethic of education. Many of these folks, having been denied the opportunity to succeed economically in the past, are hungry for success today. This has already caused quite a bit of global economic change and it is probably a safe bet that this change will continue into the future.

### So What Do We Tell Our Kids?

In a competitive global economy, there will be plenty of good jobs for people with the right skills, knowledge, and self-motivation to seize them. But our kids need to know that they will be competing with not just the kid next door, but kids in China, India, and other countries of the world. To keep our standard of living rising, we will need to move more quickly and work smarter than in the past.

It was never a good thing to be mediocre in your job, but in past years, one could be mediocre and still earn a decent wage. In a global economy, you really do not want to be mediocre at what you do...there are people all over the world that would like to have your job.

# CHAPTER 11

## *Information Systems And The Flat-world*

Let's jump right into information systems and the flat-world.

Investment in information technology during the 1990s was one of the contributing factors to unprecedented gains in productivity in the United States during the early 2000s. College graduates today are expected to be knowledgeable about computer applications and to be ready to participate in the planning and the implementation of information systems.

It is very different to be a user of **information technology (IT)** in an e-world than it was to be a computer user prior to an easy-to-use browser to navigate across Web sites. Managing IT in business today is very different from managing IT in a pre-browser business environment. We can define information technology as computer hardware and software used for processing and storing information, and communications technology used for transmitting information. Think of IT as capturing, manipulating, presenting, communicating, using and transforming data into information. You might need to refer to the decision-making section in Chapter 3 to refresh your memory on the difference between data and information.

The information systems department in most organizations has the responsibility of managing the firm's IT assets: hardware, software, networks, and information systems professionals. As the technologies grow, information system's responsibilities continue to evolve.

Some business managers see information technology only as a tool. The smart manager sees IT as integral to business and wants to know all about the key elements and tradeoffs. The idea is to make information technology a part of the organization, so that the organization is either more efficient, more effective, or both.

### Information and Risk

The risk of an incorrect decision declines as managers have more accurate information at their disposal for use in making the decision. More information means less decision risk – *decision risk* is the risk of an error in decision making. In theory, with complete and accurate information, there is no risk at all in making decisions. At the other extreme, making a decision without any information or with inaccurate information is a gamble. Decisions are typically made in business with some information that is fairly accurate, but not all the information is available to reduce decision risk to zero. Why? The answer is cost, time, and uncertainty. First, there is a tradeoff between the cost of accumulating the information and the cost of making a decision error. Second, given more time – more information could be gathered – so there is a tradeoff between the time required to gather information and the timing of the decision. A decision put off too long may have little or no value – no matter how accurate it is. Finally, for many decisions, accurate and sufficient information is simply not available at any cost or with any amount of time spent accumulating information. It could also be that the decision makers do not know enough to even be certain of what information is needed to make the decision, and how to tell what information is accurate and what information is inaccurate.

What is certain is that when the amount of available (accurate) information is high, decision makers tend to make better decisions. When the amount of information is low, decision quality tends to be poor.

### Information (Also called decision rules) Rules

Experienced business people use information rules to simplify or quicken all types of tasks and decisions. Business people try to accumulate information rules to shorten the time that they spend analyzing choices and to improve decision quality. Information rules must evolve over time, because the environment in which the decision maker operates is constantly changing.

### The Importance of Information Technology

Information technologies are critical to advancing productivity and innovation in all areas of an economy. The more an educated population is connected to the flat-world platform in an affordable and efficient way, the greater the occurrence of productivity gains and innovation. If the flat-world platform greatly improves productivity and innovation gains…but a population lacks the education or infrastructure to use it…then sooner or later (and later is a lot closer to sooner than it used to be), that population will fall behind its competitors. These populations could be an organization, a state, or a country. Even a certain population inside an organization or subgroups in states or countries could fall behind other parts of the population.

### Integrating the Arts with Math and Science

The supposed American education advantage is that we stress creativity (the arts) and not rote -learning. Other countries like China and Japan have more rote-oriented learning systems. Americans have a kind of self-confidence that whatever our population lacks in math and science, we can make up for by being independent, creative thinkers. There is some truth to this. But, a person needs to understand things in order to create beyond them. This means that a strong foundation (some rote-learning) coupled with the arts (independent thinking and creativity) can create a competitive advantage for a person or a population.

## The Flat World

Using information technologies, anyone, anywhere in the world can create, innovate, and compete. The frictions of oceans and physical distance no longer protect us from competitors all over the world. Anything that can be digitized can be outsourced to either the smartest, best, or cheapest producer.

*Work that can be moved around will get moved around. This will force everyone to focus on what their value-add really is.*

**Digitization** is the process whereby music, video, data, words, pictures, etc. are turned into bits and bytes…combinations of 1s and 0s…that can be stored on a microprocessor, manipulated on a computer screen, or transmitted over fiber-optic cables and satellites.

Let's review some of the factors that have helped to flatten the world:

1. The **World Wide Web and the Internet**: The Internet is a network of networks basically comprised of computers and cables that can deliver packets of information to anywhere in the world. The World Wide Web is like an imaginary storehouse of information. The Web exists because of programs that communicate between computers on the Internet. Without the Internet, there could not be a Web. On the Internet, you find computers, and on the Web, you find information – videos, sounds, documents, etc. The Web made the Internet useful because people that are interested in knowledge, information, communication, and collaboration don't have to know all that much about computers and cables. As discussed earlier in this section, an easy-to-install and easy-to-use browser really popularized the Internet and the Web as tools for connectivity and economic activity. Not to mention that the cables are better than they used to be - fiber-optic cables are strands of optically pure glass that are arranged in bundles. These cables can carry digitized packets of information over long distances

at the speed of light. And, because the optical fibers are so thin, a cable has many fibers allowing much more to be sent at a lower cost. Add all of this together, and you get a brand new global platform for collaboration. This all came together in the mid to late 90s, and people started to sense that things were changing in a big way.

    a.   **Uploading** is a form of collaboration in the flat world. It allows each of us to become a producer rather than just a consumer. The systems are designed for users to produce, not just consume. An example of uploading is *podcasting (the audio version of blogging)*: individuals offering songs, videos, literature, and commentary via the Internet and Web to the entire world...while cutting out the music stores and traditional content providers.

    b.   It has been long assumed that producing a product of complexity or substance takes some kind of hierarchical organization or institution. The idea was that you needed top-down vertical integration (creating value vertically) to get complicated things produced and distributed around the world. Uploading allows an individual or small group to produce really complicated things with much less money than ever before and with much less hierarchy. This idea of **creating value collaboratively or horizontally** is very different from **creating value vertically**. Some of our organizations and institutions may be obsolete...we just do not know it yet.

    c.   **From one to many** has been the typical business model, in which one producer sells to many buyers (one produces and many buy). The new business model is that you involve your customers and supply chain partners in an ongoing conversation about every aspect of your business, from product conception and design, to the supply chain that makes and delivers the product, to how the business collects and uses customer feedback, to responding quickly to changing consumer tastes.

2. **Outsourcing**: Any business activity that can be digitized can be sourced to the best, cheapest, most efficient, or smartest provider, anywhere in the world. Outsourcing is a whole new form of collaboration and horizontal value creation made possible by the PC, the Internet, and fiber-optic cable. Outsourcing means taking a specific and limited function that a company is currently doing in-house, such as call centers or accounts payable, and having another company perform that activity for you. Then you integrate the outsourced work back into your company.

3. **Offshoring**: A company takes a factory that it is operating in a place such as the American mid-west, and moves the whole thing to another country like China or India. There, the plant produces the very same product with the very same processes.

4. **Global Supply Chaining**: Supply chaining is a way of collaborating horizontally among suppliers, retailers, and customers to create value in the marketplace. It is easy with today's technology to reverse-engineer any product and be able to make it in a short period of time…this means *making stuff* is easy compared to making a process that *delivers stuff* across the globe. Supply chains are all about delivering a product to the customer at the lowest total delivered cost. A positive side effect of good supply chaining is that the quality of products will also go up. So…the consumer gets a better product…at a lower cost…think Wal-Mart. Wal-Mart does not make anything it sells, but what it does "make" is a very efficient supply chain. This is not only hard to do, but is also very hard to duplicate. Good supply chaining has to do two things: (1) get the most reliable, low cost delivery system in place; and (2) coordinate disruption-prone supply with hard-to-predict demand. The shortening product life cycles of products makes getting these two things done all the more difficult.

**Replacing inventory with information** is about using IT to get information from stores about what consumers are buying (styles, colors, etc.) back into the supply chain so that the best adjustments can be made sooner. In addition, accurate information about products in the supply chain allows for lower inventory levels, while maintaining service levels to the customer. Efficient supply chains can also produce and deliver products faster, thereby lowering the need for inventory.

5. **Searching – Google, etc.**: Never before in the history of the world have so many people had the ability to find and access so much information. With searching, we can find what we want, on our own, no matter how obscure. People can produce more obscure things and buyers can find them. Searching is empowering for individuals; it is the opposite of being told or taught.
    a. Companies are thriving not by pushing products on their customers, but by building collaborative systems that enable customers to pull on their own…then the company responds fast to what its buyers pull (see the end of Chapter 1 for a review of push and pull).
    b. Standard TV is one producer to many buyers (one to many), but now with TiVo, you can become your own TV editor. TiVo allows us to digitally record what we want and skip the ads if we want. We can watch what we want, and when we want, no need to follow a TV channel's schedule or watch commercials that are usually forced upon us.

6. The **fall of the Soviet Empire**: This tipped the balance of power to those advocating democratic and free-market oriented economies across the world. Market oriented economies are governed more by the demands, interests, and goals of the people, instead of a top down system that rules by and for the interests of some narrow ruling group. Communism is a fabulous system for making people equally poor. In contrast, capitalism makes people unequally wealthy. Free markets set

the stage for horizontal value creation among people all over the globe. Communism did not allow for collaboration among people within its own countries, let alone with people in other countries. Today it is increasingly difficult for a country to remain reclusive and hostile.

## Now That the World Is Flat

Power and wealth will increasingly go to those individuals, companies, groups, and countries that can do the following:

1. That have good infrastructure to connect to the flat-world platform.
2. That possess the education, skills, and culture to get their populations using, innovating, and collaborating from the platform.
3. That have created good governance systems to get the best from the platform and to cushion any bad side effects.

# CHAPTER 12

## *Today's Business And Conclusion*

A business has to continually ask (and answer) three questions:
o   **What is the nature of the industry in which we compete?**
o   **Where is our business (and industry) headed?**
o   **How can we make money in this business?**

Answering these questions realistically can be tough. In the past, sellers could get by with marginal performance. Today, the business environment is much less forgiving of mistakes and lack of performance. The demand for precision and excellence in business is increasing. And, as always, there are sellers that are figuring out how to deliver more precision and excellence.

We want to know what the world is really like so that we can successfully deal with it. Dealing with the world in a way that is based on how we want it to be will not be as effective. We will not get the results that we want.

### Organizing Around Outcomes and Not Tasks
What should come first...specific financial targets, or business strategy? The financial targets are the desired outcome. Once these are determined and are in balance with the external environment and

internal capabilities, then a business strategy and processes can be created to achieve the outcomes.

Sometimes an organization (and individuals, too) becomes so focused on processes that it forgets about the outcomes: creating value for customers, owners, and employees.

*The purpose of a process(s) is to achieve an outcome(s) (or a goal; a priority). Processes should not dictate outcomes... Desired outcomes should determine the processes...*

## The Need for Faster and More Frequent Change
*Later is a lot closer to sooner than it used to be...*
Sellers increasingly find themselves dealing with external environmental forces that they did not see coming. To successfully manage external threats and take advantage of opportunities, sellers will need to adjust (change) faster and more frequently. Change must be the right change - change that improves the mix of the company's business model so that value is created for customers, owners, and employees. The businessperson must know what part of the business model needs to change and what part needs to be left alone.

*The more change that an organization can handle, the more freedom a seller has in adjusting its business model.*

Sometimes business people refuse to face a new reality and avoid change no matter what the cost. Just as damaging is change for the sake of change...a problem or new reality is observed that demands action...and action (change) is made...but the change does nothing to improve the seller's business model. Value is not created for customers, owners, and employees. So, a question that can be asked is:

*Does the change (or not changing) help to create a more robust business model that delivers more value to customers, owners, and employees?*

Remember, you cannot have one without the others (for very long). If more value is delivered to customers, owners, and employees, then the change (or not changing) is good.

A seller can use its business model to anticipate external environmental realities and then make realistic changes that will create positive outcomes. But, the good news must actually be good news... sometimes people develop a bias toward hearing good news. We like good news and want to avoid bad news. It is easy to start filtering out (a perceptual screen) the bad news and hear only what we want to hear. A strong seller can look at itself in the mirror and be honest about what needs to change...and then make the commitment and successfully execute positive change.

Sometimes a seller does not want to disrupt itself with change...it instead hopes the new challenges or opportunities will go away. The problem is that there is always a seller somewhere that will embrace the challenge or opportunity. This seller will move forward with a robust business model that creates value for customers, owners, and employees. Other sellers will be left behind with obsolete business models that no longer deliver value. Thus, a seller that refuses to disrupt itself when change is needed will always end up being disrupted by problems caused by the lack of value creation, or an imbalance in its business model. Its business model is not sustainable.

Anticipating what is on the horizon and acting on it can bring large rewards for a seller. Waiting too long to take action will reduce a seller's options, choices, and outcomes. There are plenty of smart business people around the world that are ready and willing to try new and different things to gain a competitive edge and earn the customer's business. Companies that stick with old practices and behaviors will find it increasingly difficult to satisfy the customer.

**Globalization**
Even businesses that were previously considered local, too small, or too specialized are being impacted by globalization. Some of the reasons for this are:

o The Internet speeds the flow of data, information, and ideas to all corners of the globe. This leads to more creativity and faster decision-making. So many things now move and happen so much faster than ever before in history. Communication between sellers, buyers, countries, cultures, and individuals is many times better and faster than ever before.

o Capital (money) is much more mobile than ever before in history. Large, worldwide over-investment coupled with excess capacity in many industries has resulted in excess supply in relation to demand. This has resulted in a shift of power from owners and managers of capital to consumers and marketing intermediaries such as Wal-Mart.

o New and unexpected competition can come from anywhere in the world…at any time…and without warning. Practically all business activities are likely to have some sort of worldwide dimension.

o The fast and efficient flow of data, information, and ideas has resulted in ever-shortening product life cycles. What is a differentiated product today with a nice margin can quickly become a commodity with a very low or even negative margin for sellers with higher costs.

o Improved transportation and distribution systems can move products around the world quickly and efficiently.

o Ever-improving global supply chains seek out the best worldwide sources of supply.

o There are now fewer economic frictions between countries and cultures, which then results in increased integration of business activity across countries and cultures.

o Consumer expectations have changed: consumers demand (and receive) better quality and more choices at lower prices. Sellers must perform, with no failures. Dissatisfied consumers can always switch to another seller that will perform.

**Doing What We Know Best**

A big mistake is that when things change, people and organizations often do not contemplate how they need to change or adapt to the new environment. Instead, they double their efforts doing what they know best. Heroic efforts are made…but many times these efforts are pointless, because they ignore the current market conditions (realities).

Many managers today are fighting yesterday's fight. When faced with intense worldwide price competition, they try to reduce costs by cutting expenses, closing plants, consolidating plants, reducing the workforce, consolidating companies, and so on. These actions might work if the pressure on margins was coming from domestic competitors or cyclical economic forces. But what we are experiencing today is **structural change**. This means how a business will make money in the future will change. **In today's business, you have to have global cost parity**. Cost parity means that a seller cannot be out of line with the lowest-cost worldwide source.

A few things that can cause a businessperson or business trouble are:

o Hearing what we want hear. This could be caused by not facing a problem, either because we cannot see a solution to it, or because of past experience, preconceived opinions and thoughts, or even arrogance from past success.

o Receiving filtered information from sources that are biased, have an agenda, or simply think just like you do. It is important to get information at the source that is not distorted and is from different points of view.

o Thinking that it is going to work "because we need it to work."

o Unrealistic expectations of money-making. Everyone wants the pie to get bigger…faster…with less effort…and with less thinking.

o Emotions come into play. Deeply committed people can do great things…but sometimes an emotional over-investment can lead to ignoring reality.

It appears that avoiding reality is a basic human tendency. In a command society, it is a necessity for survival. However it is something that people choose to do in open societies. In private life, we can be forced into unrealism to keep the peace in marriages, families and organized activities. The same thing can occur when one is at work. Sometimes it seems that there is no choice. There are areas of public life where unreality is accepted or even expected. Examples are movies, TV, sports, institutions, and even some government policy making.

*Business people and businesses do have the choice to be either realistic or unrealistic. Being realistic requires some courage…a curious mind… an open mind…a questioning mind…and the intellectual discipline to sort through complexity.*

### The Global Economy
All of this adds up to fantastic opportunities for those that develop a clear understanding of what is happening, and can create business models to adapt to the opportunities. One must be able to determine whether change is cyclical or structural. Competent business people can deal with cyclical change. In the early stages, structural change can look a lot like cyclical change. But this is the time when companies need to see the structural changes…it is harder to adjust if they wait for the structural change to become obvious.

### Comparative Advantage
Classic economics says that a country can have a comparative advantage over other countries if it has an edge of some kind in one or more of the factors of production: natural resources, labor, financial capital, and entrepreneurship. Remember that entrepreneurship is the willingness to take risks and the knowledge and skills necessary to use the other three factors efficiently. This is also called social or intellectual capital.

Natural resources and labor are hard to move. But the factors of production that matter the most today are financial capital and knowledge. These two factors can be quickly moved to anywhere in the world by modern technology (at the speed of light in a fiber-optic cable) and, compared to past decades, are relatively unconstrained in their movement by frictions. This changes how we must think about comparative advantage.

### Structurally Defective Industries

Structurally defective industries are industries that are so impacted by structural change that there are no obvious solutions. A company in a structurally defective industry is chronically unable to be successful at money-making. Cutting costs and consolidating companies does not solve the real problems these sellers face. It only creates a larger struggling business. To be a talented employee in such an industry can be misery. These companies have obsolete business models.

### The Business Model

A seller must be clear about its organizational culture and capabilities. It must understand its industry. The plans it makes and the goals it sets must be realistic. It needs a strong business model. A critical step is **reducing complexity to its simplest expression without being simplistic**. From this comes the business model and business priorities (goals, outcomes)…the priorities must be clear and simple, and the clear, simple message must be repeated often. And, the business model must evolve over time so that it can continue to deliver value to owners, customers, and employees.

### Know the Final Customer – the End User

In assessing the business model, knowledge of the customer is the most valuable of all the external information that can be gathered. If a seller knew everything there was to know about the customers' current and future wants and needs, the external environment would hold fewer surprises. Maintaining good margins requires that a seller differentiate its product from competitors' offerings. The only way a seller can differentiate its product is to know the people to whom it wants to sell better and in a more timely way than anyone else. This means knowing all the customers in the distribution channel (see the supply chain in Chapter 7), and particularly the final consumer.

This kind of knowledge comes from viewing your own business from the end user's perspective. What do we look like through the end user's eyes? What does the end user really need, want, and value? How much is the end user willing to pay?

## The decision of what to make and sell starts with the final customer.

To succeed in a highly competitive world market, the seller has to understand the customer better than ever before, understand what the customer is willing to pay, and then work backward to offer a mix of physical goods, tangible services, and psychological services (from Chapter 7) that deliver value to the customer…and differentiates the product from competitors. The concept of physical goods and services grouped together into a product helps us focus on providing all the elements that the customer wants or needs…seeing the product as the customer sees it.

The differentiation must be things that really matter to the final customer. A forward-looking view is needed to anticipate what customers will need and want; because speed counts…customers don't like to wait. Sometimes the customer will not understand their own needs and wants…particularly future needs and wants. The seller can create a differential advantage by taking the time and making the effort to completely understand the customer. This is called outside-in thinking, or the customer chain.

A skill that is becoming increasingly more important is a curiosity… a desire to learn about what is new and different. Such a person has a desire to relentlessly search for information that can make a difference for the business. This person searches for new ideas and new ways of doing things from diverse sources of information. They don't rely on past assumptions, nor do they take anything for granted. They create scenarios (stories) in their minds that capitalize on opportunities or effectively deal with threats. I have heard some people call this strategic dreaming…it is future storytelling.

**Conclusion**

So now we have finished learning "How a Business Works" in 12 chapters. At this point, I would encourage you to look at the Preface again. Remember that the goal of this book was to create a framework for understanding business. Try to think about business using this framework, and it will serve you in the following ways:

1. It will help you to understand the behavior of sellers and employers, so that you can be a more informed businessperson, citizen, consumer, and employee.

2. It will help you to predict the future behavior of sellers and employers, so that you can make better plans and achieve better outcomes as a businessperson, citizen, consumer, and employee.

3. It will give you a basic understanding of business (a framework), so that you can effectively and efficiently learn more about business and organizations from the perspective of your roles: as a citizen, as a consumer, as an employee, and possibly as a businessperson.

The framework that you have developed will help you in answering questions that you have relating to business. This framework is a powerful tool and ally in figuring out what questions to ask, and then in answering them or being able to seek out the appropriate resource for answers.

Finally, this is not the end, but the beginning. Just like business, we as individuals need to be continuously improving so that we will be prepared for the opportunities and demands of the future. I encourage you to use your newly developed framework to continue to learn more about business from the perspectives of your various roles. I wish you success in your ongoing study of Business.

# Appendix 1

## Norton and West Certified Public Accountants, L.L.C.
### A Business Case

### Forward for the Case

The primary purpose of this business case is to give you an overall picture of an actual business. While I have made up this business, everything that you will see is a mirror of the real world. The first business case, Midwest Aluminum at the end of Chapter 6, was a manufacturing company. Norton and West is a service business. One big difference that you will notice immediately is the amount of cost of goods sold on the functional format income statement. For a service business, cost of goods sold is a small percentage of sales revenue. The big expenditure for an accounting firm is people cost – the accountants and the staff. The people cost for an accounting firm is essentially a fixed cost. This fact appears on the contribution format income statement – fixed expenses are a large proportion of total expenses.

I have purposely used a small business, so that it is easier to get a picture of the entire business. Try to get a picture in your mind, and then see how it fits in the framework that we have developed for understanding business. The idea is to use this business case to put the final touches on the framework that you have developed.

### Norton and West Certified Public Accountants, L.L.C.

Norton and West Certified Public Accountants, L.L.C. was founded as a public accounting firm 15 years ago by Steve Norton and Carol West (the members).

The members invested $50,000 each into the new business for a total of $100,000. The firm was originally a *partnership*, in which Norton and West were known as the *partners*, but the firm has since been reformed as a *limited liability company*, so now Norton and West are known as the *members*.

### Background

A certified *public accounting* firm provides accounting services to the public. The services provided by Norton and West CPAs are listed in the services section in this case. In contrast, *private accounting* provides accounting services to an employer. Thus there are two main categories of accounting: public and private accounting. The two are very different. Public accountants work with outside customers, usually called clients. Public accountants must do their work within the guidelines of their profession and, at the same time, keep their customers satisfied. A public accountant works daily with clients and must constantly be focused on customer service and customer satisfaction. A component of customer satisfaction is the cost of the accounting services to the client. If Norton and West's fees become too high, the customers will move their business to a competing public accounting firm that is more competitively priced. What this all means to Steve and Carol is that *they must keep their business operating costs under control. As business managers, they must be both efficient and effective.*

Steve Norton has a Bachelor of Science degree in accounting from Indiana University. He successfully passed all four sections of the CPA exam while working for a large public accounting firm in Indianapolis, Indiana. At Norton and West, Steve specializes in tax and small business accounting.

Carol West specializes in litigation and auditing. She received her Bachelor of Science degree from Purdue University in accounting. After graduation, she worked at a large public accounting firm in Chicago, Illinois, and during this time successfully passed all four sections of the CPA exam.

The firm occupies a 4,500 square foot office in Greenwood, Indiana. The firm primarily seeks business customers. Typically, the firm will also do the client's personal tax and accounting work. As a result, even though the firm does not actively seek personal tax return work, the firm does approximately 700 personal tax returns per year. Personal tax returns are not a great moneymaker. The minimum fee for a personal return is $240 for the very simplest return at Norton and West. In contrast, a competitor for personal tax return work is H & R Block – which is a very different service. H & R Block charges $125 to $200 for simple personal tax returns. The usual fee at Norton and West for a personal tax return is about $350.

In public accounting, members of limited liability companies and partners for partnerships must be certified public accountants. To become a *certified public accountant* (CPA), a person must complete 150 hours of undergraduate college course work, obtain a bachelor's degree (a four year college degree), have several years of experience in public accounting at a CPA firm, and pass the CPA exam. The exam consists of four sections. Each section of the exam takes on average 4 ½ hours to complete. Once a person has passed a section of the exam, they need not take it again. For example, if a person took the exam and passed two sections, they would only be required to retake the two sections that they did not pass. Only eight percent of exam takers pass all four sections on the first try. It is a tough exam.

The other accountants on the professional accounting staff may or may not be certified public accountants, as they work under the supervision of the managing CPAs. The professional accounting staff is, however, expected to be pursuing the passing of the CPA exam.

### The Industry
The public accounting industry is characterized by a seasonal workload caused by tax season. The busiest time of the year is from January to April 15. Summer is the slowest time. Things begin heating up again in October, as firms prepare for tax season.

Norton and West CPAs use *flex time* to help even out the seasonal workload. Everyone works more hours during tax season, but fewer hours during the summer. The type of person that would like public accounting is one that likes this arrangement – busy January thru April 15, and extra free time during the summer.

### In-Charge List

Either Norton or West will make up an "in-charge list" for each client based on the client's needs. The member will specify which individuals from the professional staff and paraprofessional staff will be assigned to do the client's work. This is a critical managerial task, as the member must correctly analyze the work to be done, and then apply that analysis to the organization to produce the most efficient in-charge list. Efficiency is defined in this case as having the work done by the lowest billing rate person that is qualified to do the work. To do this, the member must understand the organization and its individuals very well and have a clear picture of the overall workload of the organization and of each individual. Each individual in the firm has certain things that they do better than others. In addition, the organization as a whole has certain strengths and weaknesses. The organization's ability to do work varies as the people in the organization change with new hires and people leaving the firm, and as the people within the firm improve their skills. This means that the firm's production system is different from year to year, even if there are no changes in personnel. Add to this the inevitable changes in personnel, and the firm becomes a constantly changing production system with ever-changing capacities and capabilities.

The in-charge list does not always include someone from each level of the professional staff and paraprofessional staff. It could even include two or more people from the same level. The mix of the in-charge list will depend on the needs of the client and the overall demand on the production system.

We can think of the in-charge list as having these objectives:

o Achieve client satisfaction by completing the client's work at an acceptable quality level, which for an accounting firm means minimizing external failures (errors). Completing work on time is also of critical importance.

o Keep the client's billings at acceptable (to the client) levels by having the lowest billing-rate person qualified to do each activity do that activity.

o Maintain high utilization rates for each person and for the organization; otherwise, the firm's operating costs will be too high.

o Produce a profit for the firm.

o Allow the members to plan, lead, and control the service to each client.

o Strive to be effective and efficient. The two members must also combine their efforts to be effective and efficient as a team.


**Services**

The firm offers the following services to clients

o Accounting

o Tax

o Auditing

o Management and consulting

o Administration of qualified retirement plans

o Business valuation

o Data processing


The services are generally billed to clients based on time. Each accountant or

paraprofessional's hours on a job are added and multiplied by that individual's billing rate. The sum of each person on the in-charge list would then equal the amount billed to the client. Since services are billed by the hour, the most efficient in-charge list would have each activity for a client done by the lowest billing-rate person that is qualified to do the work. To keep clients, the firm must hold the client's accounting costs down.

The firm's hourly billing rates are as follows: members - $140; managers - $95; supervisors - $82; senior accountants - $73; staff accountants - $64; and paraprofessionals - $36. For billing purposes, each accountant keeps track of their time in six-minute intervals throughout each day. A summary is made at the end of each week.

### The Organization

The firm is organized with a *professional staff*, a *paraprofessional staff*, a *support staff*, and a *professional support staff*. The firm also has a summer intern and a winter/spring intern. The *interns* are usually in their junior or senior year in college and have completed a considerable amount of accounting coursework. The summer internship is a full-time position for three months, and the winter/spring internship is part-time, usually about 15 hours per week, for nine months. The internships pay $16 per hour.

The professional staff comprises the majority of the people in the firm. The professional staff members must possess a Bachelor's degree and be pursuing the successful passing of the CPA exam. The professional staff is paid by salary. At Norton and West CPAs, the starting position is called a staff accountant. In two to three years a person may be promoted to senior accountant. A person must serve as a senior accountant at least two years before they can be promoted to a supervisor position. After supervisor, the next position is called manager, and after manager is the very top of the organization – member.

Norton and West CPAs is considered a small firm. Salaries vary depending on the size of the firm, with larger firms paying higher salaries and smaller firms paying lower salaries. For small accounting firms, the salary ranges per year are generally as follows: staff accountant with up to one year of experience - $29,500 to $36,250; staff accountant with one to three years of experience - $33,750 to 42,500; senior accountant - $41,000 to $54,000; supervisor - $52,000 to $66,000; and manager - $63,750 to $84,500. Exact salaries are based on experience, skills, competencies, work quality, and the possession of the CPA designation.

The paraprofessional staff is paid by the hour and must possess an Associate's degree (a two year college degree). Norton and West CPAs pay its two paraprofessionals $14 per hour.

The support staff has no particular educational or certification requirements, but experience and skill at working with clients is very important. At Norton and West CPA's, the support staff is paid an average of $11 per hour.

The professional support staff is paid by salary, and generally requires a Bachelor's degree. In addition, the human resources manager must possess several HR certifications. At Norton and West CPAs, the professional staff consists of a business and human resources manager, a part-time marketing manager (10 hours per week), and a part-time systems manager (2 days per week).

See Exhibit 1 for the firm's organizational chart.

### Operations – Process

The accounting firm is a *batch process* (discussed in Chapter 7). Work flows from accountant to accountant in a jumbled sequence. The process is very flexible, but work can build up at an accountant's workstation (desk). The firm attempts to reduce work in process inventory by the following method. Each week, everyone in the firm fills out a workload sheet. The human resources manager reviews each person's workload sheet and reallocates work from overloaded employees to employees with lower workloads. This sounds fine (and is a necessity), but the reallocation could change the in-charge list and the efficiency of the production system (lowest billing person does the work). The decisions by the human resources manager are efficiency decisions, and thus will impact the original efficiency decisions made by the member. Fortunately for the firm, the HR manager is a very experienced person, having worked as an accountant at the firm for six years before assuming the responsibilities of HR manager.

The in-charge list outlines the exact flow of each client's work. Since each client's in-charge list is different (because of different needs), the flow of work for each client will be different – thus the batch flow process.

### Operations - Quality Systems

The main objective of each of the firm's quality systems is to minimize *external failures*. The firm desires to find errors internally - these are called *internal failures*. The advantage of internal failures over external failures is that customers and clients never see the error or loss of quality. Only those working within the organization will know that an error has occurred. Also, errors are much easier and less costly to correct when they are still at the place of business and under the complete control of the accountants.

The accounting firm's primary quality system is that everything done in the firm is checked by at least one other qualified person. Thus, each accountant spends a given amount of time each week checking the work of coworkers. Besides coworkers, the accountants also rely on their computer software. The software programs are designed to look for inconsistencies in the work and possible errors. If the software detects an inconsistency or possible error, it will signal with an error message to the accountant. The accountant then rechecks that area to correct errors or to ensure that no error has been made.

Next, all work is checked by the support staff to guarantee that all work has a professional appearance and is consistent with the firm's "look."

In the final step, one of the members reviews the work and signs it. The work is now ready to leave the firm. The bill can now be completed and sent to the client.

**Operations – Capacity**

The firm's capacity can be defined as the total number of hours that the firm can bill to clients. The total possible billing hours are constrained by the number of people working for the firm, and the efficiency of the firm. Within the total hours, the billing rates for different levels vary, which will impact both revenue and operating expenses. See Exhibit 2 to see the firm's billing potential and billing efficiency.

Since the flow of work in the firm is a batch flow, the sequencing of work (scheduling) by each accountant is of great importance. The question is always, "what job should I work on next?" The question can be answered by using *dispatch rules*. Dispatch rules decide which job should be next from a queue (group) of jobs. Some examples of dispatch rules for batch processes are as follows:

- o First come, first served – is based on the familiar fairness criterion, where the job that arrives first at a work center is first to be processed.
- o Minimum processing time – the job with the shortest processing time at the workstation will be processed next. The idea here is that workstations downstream will benefit by receiving work when a job is finished quickly. This results in a high flow rate and high utilization of the production system.
- o Minimum slack time per operation – *slack time* is defined as the time remaining until the due date minus the processing time remaining. Thus, the jobs that are the closest to being late on the due date (completion time) will be done next.
- o Minimum due date – the job with the closest due date is processed next.
- o Minimum processing time with truncation – the job with the shortest processing time is selected next, just as in the minimum processing time rule. The exception is when a job has waited a specified period of time. The rule is then truncated; the job that has been waiting longest is done next.
- o Critical ratio – the critical ratio is remaining time until due date divided by remaining processing time. The job with the lowest critical ratio is completed next.

### Operations – Inventory

Because an accounting firm is close to being a *pure service* provider, the firm has little physical goods in what it sells to clients. This means that the firm has little *raw material inventory* and no *finished goods inventory*. *Work-in-process inventory* is another story. Since the flow of work is jumbled, there is a tendency for work-in-process inventory to build up. In this case, work-in-process inventory is work that accountants have in jobs, but the job is not yet complete and ready to send out to the client (and be billed).

Thus, two important managerial tasks for the members are:
1. Efficient loading of the production system to maintain good work flows and achieve a high utilization rate of the available capacity
2. Hold down work-in-process inventory

### Solving Production Problems

The firm uses an operations technique called *process flow analysis* to solve its production problems and bottlenecks. Process flow analysis is a tool used to analyze how the product is made. The firm then develops written guidelines for the process.

### Marketing

Norton and West CPAs must add new clients to replace lost clients. Clients may go out of business, switch to a competing CPA firm, or pass away. To grow, the firm must find more new clients than it loses in current clients.

Don May is the marketing manager. He is semi-retired, and a long-time resident of Greenwood. He works about 10 hours per week marketing the firm's services primarily by *personal selling*. Don spends about 60% of his time *prospecting* for new clients. He has about 100 prospects in various stages of development. Some potential clients can take years to become clients. Don knows his job is about persistence

– he will keep calling on a potential client unless asked to stop. Many of Don's prospects come through referrals – from his many contacts that he has developed over the years. He uses sources such as the local chamber of commerce, banks, and other professional services. Sometimes he *cold calls* from the chamber of commerce membership book.

Don has found that living, shopping, playing, and having kids in the community is a big help in marketing. He encourages the firm's accounting interns to take some marketing courses along with their accounting courses before completing their Bachelor's degree. He sees this as necessary because everyone in the firm (the *marketing concept*) must market the firm's services for the firm to be successful in the highly competitive market of professional accounting services. However, the members are considering a different marketing strategy when Don retires completely in a few years. Rather than have a marketing director, the members think that they could encourage the accountants to sell the firm's services by paying the accountant that lands a new client a fee equal to 10% of the first year's billings and a fee of 5% of the billings thereafter. The fees would be in addition to the accountant's regular salary. Does this sound like a good idea to you?

Besides prospecting, Don calls on the firm's present clients to fish for information such as how satisfied the clients are with the firm's work, billing amounts, and timeliness of work. This activity provides Don with much needed marketing feedback, as well as providing additional quality control information.

Finally, Don thinks that public accounting is going to move more to consulting and away from traditional accounting services because of software. In other words, advances in software will change the product(s) that accountants sell. As software does more and more of the traditional accounting services, accountants must seek to find new services that they can offer clients. Consulting is an obvious choice. Thus, the firm's *product mix* will evolve over time in response to changes in technology.

Since everyone in the firm markets the firm's services to some degree, marketing costs are not listed separately on the firm's income statement (see exhibits).

### Matching Supply and Demand

One of the toughest things to get right in business is to match *supply* and *demand*. If the firm has more capacity to produce accounting services than is necessary to meet the demand for those services, the firm's costs will be too high. Efficiency will be low, which will result either in the firm losing money, or its prices being too high, or both.

If the firm has less capacity than is needed to meet demand, several things could happen. The firm may have to turn away customers, which would mean lost sales revenue...and potential customers lost today may never return as clients. The firm could try to increase its output in the short run by everyone working harder and longer hours. The outcome of this strategy will usually be higher operating costs, lower overall productivity, missed due dates (and unhappy clients), quality problems (and again, unhappy clients), and lowered organizational morale. By adding a few too many clients and overloading the production system, the firm could lose the confidence of all its customers. Overloading will not just affect the last few clients, but it will affect all the clients through the above-mentioned problems, and could actually reduce the firm's overall profitability.

Either *scenario* of unmatched supply and demand is unpleasant. This matching is difficult because demand is constantly changing. The ability to supply accounting services is also constantly changing as some employees leave the firm and new employees start at the firm. Also, each employee's skills and competencies are changing daily (hopefully improving), which will affect the organization's production capacity. Finally, environmental factors, such as changes in technology (particularly software) and governmental activities (particularly changes in the tax law), can change the firm's ability to supply accounting services. Environmental factors that can change demand include things such as competitors' activities, technology (particularly software), social and cultural changes, economic factors, and government (particularly changes in the tax law).

Experienced business managers will seek to match supply and demand closely enough to maintain an efficient organization, keep costs under control, keep clients satisfied, and produce a profit.

### Human Resources

Because Norton and West CPAs is a small firm, Ralph York wears several hats in the office. He serves as business manager, office manager, and human resources manager. He stays very busy.

When hiring a new employee, the firm looks for a good "fit." The members and human resources manager look for people that they think will fit in well with the current organization and will be happy in the organization. The members want to avoid hiring mistakes because the human resources manager estimates that the replacement cost to fix a hiring mistake equals 1.5 times the salary of the replaced individual.

One way the members seek to avoid hiring errors is by internships. Ralph York, the HR manager, says, "We love internships; they give us a chance to really get to know a potential employee, and in turn the person really gets to know us." Another benefit is that it makes the first year on the job much easier if a person has had an internship. All the firm's new staff accountants over the past several years have been former interns. One or sometimes two new staff accountants are hired each year.

Ralph describes the characteristics of a good public accountant. First, the individual is good with people and clients, and enjoys customer service. Second, the accountant likes precision, accuracy, numbers, and is organized. Third, the person is competent with computer systems, though there is no need to be an expert, as the firm has a systems manager. Finally, the ability to do things quickly, without mistakes, is a must.

Besides good hiring, one of Ralph's most important jobs is to ensure that all the employees of the firm have fair workloads. To that end, each employee fills out a workload sheet each week for Ralph. He reviews each person's workload and reallocates work among the employees as necessary. This reallocation, however, could change the in charge list. How does Ralph do it? Experience and skill is how. He understands the production process because he served as a staff accountant and senior accountant for six years before going into administration. Only someone with his experience could make efficient work reallocations.

The firm provides various benefits to both salaried and hourly employees. These benefits cost the firm, on average, 26% of an employee's salary or wages for a year. The benefits provided include the firm's portion of social security tax for the employee, accident and health insurance, a retirement plan, and term life insurance.

### Continuing Education

Continuing education is a requirement in public accounting. The need to maintain cutting-edge knowledge and competencies cannot be underestimated. Employees and members participate in in-house continuing education and also in external continuing ed. The firm also maintains a complete library that is used regularly by the employees.

### Information Systems

April Baldwin is the IT (information technology), or systems manager. The firm is too small to need a full-time systems manager, so April works at the firm two days per week. The other three days a week, she works at other small companies in a similar arrangement. Experience is very important in this position, as April has no one else to go to for help or to ask questions. She enjoys working for the smaller firms because with her 18 years of IT experience, she likes to invent and create. The small firm allows her to do that. In larger organizations, IT folks frequently get to do only a narrow range of activities.

April explains that a firm does not need a full-time systems manager until it has at least 40 PCs. She quips that computers are basically stupid. One cannot leave out anything in the sequence of activities to complete a task when directing a computer. This takes a certain kind of mindset and very detailed thinking. If even the simplest step is left out, the computer cannot complete the task, because the computer cannot fill in blanks or spaces on its own.

Good software really adds to the *productivity* of the accountants. For example, the firm thinks that with computer software, an accountant can prepare a tax return in half the time it took in the pre-computer days of public accounting.

**Exhibit 1 – 2007 Organizational Chart**
**Norton and West Certified Public Accountants, L.L.C.**

*Members*

Steve Norton, CPA          Carol West, CPA
($90,000)                  ($90,000)

**Professional Support Staff**
Ralph York
*Administrative Manager*
(Business, Office, & HR)
($48,000)

*Managers*

Maria Reyes
($77,000)

Don May
*Marketing Manager*
(Part-time $12,000)

*Supervisors*

Jill Ashton, CPA          George Williams
($63,000)                 ($57,000)

April Baldwin
*Systems Manager*
(Part-time $25,000)

*Senior Accountants*

Ricardo Alvarez, CPA      Cindy Howard
($51,000)                 ($46,000)

**College Interns**

Vickie Banks
*Summer Intern*
($16 hr / $5,600)

*Staff Accountants*

Linda Eads                Richard Conner
($36,000)                 ($40,000)

David Taft                Laura Wilson
($39,000)                 ($41,000)

Roberto Gomez
*Fall/Spring Intern*
($16 hr / $8,400)
Part - time-9 months

*Paraprofessionals*

Melissa Roberts           Grant Henderson
($14 hr / $28,000)        ($14 hr / $28,000)

*Support Staff*

Catherine Steel           John Donnelly
($11 hr / $22,000)        ($11 hr / $22,000)

Note: ($) under name indicates annual salary or wages.

**Exhibit 2 – Maximum Billing Capacity for 2007**
**Norton and West Certified Public Accountants, L.L.C.**

Billing potential of the firm, assuming each billable person works a 2,000 hour year.

| | *Billing Rate* | | *Hours* | *Billing Potential* |
|---|---|---|---|---|
| Members (2) | $140 | X | 4,000 = | $560,000 |
| Managers (1) | $95 | X | 2,000 = | $190,000 |
| Supervisors (2) | $82 | X | 4,000 = | $328,000 |
| Senior Accountants (2) | $73 | X | 4,000 = | $292,000 |
| Staff Accountants (4) | $64 | X | 8,000 = | $512,000 |
| Paraprofessionals (2) | $36 | X | 4,000 = | $144,000 |
| Totals | | | 26,000 | $2,026,000 |

Billing Efficiency can then be calculated for 2007 by:

Sales Revenue   divided by   Billing Potential

or

**$1,531,048  ÷  $2,026,000  =  75.57%  Billing Efficiency**

**Exhibit 3 - Income Statement for 2007 - Norton & West CPAs, LLC**

| | | | |
|---|---|---:|---:|
| **SALES REVENUE** | | $1,531,048 | 100.00% |
| | | | |
| *Cost of Sales* | | | |
| Direct costs of tax processing | 24,573 | | |
| Software and hardware | 90,325 | | |
| **Subtotal - Cost of Sales** | | (114,898) | |
| **GROSS PROFIT** | | 1,416,150 | 92.50% |
| **OPERATING EXPENSES** | | | |
| *Salaries & wages* | | | |
| Professional salaries | 793,800 | | |
| Paraprofessional wages | 70,560 | | |
| Support staff wages | 55,440 | | |
| Administrative salaries | 91,980 | | |
| Marketing salaries | 15,120 | | |
| **Subtotal - Salaries & Wages** | (1,026,900) | | |
| **Subtotal - Other Operating Expenses (Exh 4)** | (250,061) | | |
| **Total Operating Expenses** | | (1,276,961) | 83.40% |
| **NET INCOME FROM OPERATIONS** | | 139,189 | 9.09% |
| *Other Income & Expenses* | | | |
| Interest income | 2,265 | | |
| Interst expense | (15,387) | | |
| **Subtotal - Other Income & Expenses** | | (13,122) | 0.86% |
| **NET INCOME BEFORE TAXES** | | $126,067 | 8.23% |
| | | | |
| To arrive at net income after taxes, let's assume that Norton and West pay 30% of the net income before taxes of the business as personal income taxes. | | (37,820) | |
| Net Income After Taxes, or Margin | | $88,247 | 5.76% |

## Exhibit 4 - Other Expenses for the 2007 Income Statement

### Other Operating Expenses

| | |
|---|---:|
| Advertising | $3,798 |
| Bad debts | 23,392 |
| Computer repair & maintenance, supplies | 11,163 |
| Contributions | 10,618 |
| Copier | 4,971 |
| Depreciation | 35,107 |
| Dues, subscriptions, association expense | 2,709 |
| Insurance | 9,939 |
| Internet service | 2,385 |
| Janitorial services | 4,254 |
| Library, newsletters | 2,853 |
| Meals, entertainment, travel | 15,485 |
| Microfilm maintenance & supplies | 3,411 |
| Miscellaneous | 1,518 |
| Office supplies | 8,793 |
| Postage | 7,757 |
| Professional development | 27,343 |
| Professional services | 24,713 |
| Rent | 36,000 |
| Repair & maintenance - office | 1,858 |
| Telephone | 5,820 |
| Utilities | 6,174 |
| | |
| ***Subtotal - Other Operating Expenses*** | **$250,061** |

| Exhibit 5 - Income Statement for 2006 - Norton & West CPAs, LLC | | | |
|---|---|---|---|
| **SALES REVENUE** | | $1,500,427 | 100.00% |
| *Cost of Sales* | | | |
| Direct costs of tax processing | 24,991 | | |
| Software and hardware | 88,794 | | |
| **Subtotal - Cost of Sales** | | (113,785) | |
| **GROSS PROFIT** | | 1,386,642 | 92.42% |
| **OPERATING EXPENSES** | | | |
| *Salaries & wages* | | | |
| Professional salaries | 780,924 | | |
| Paraprofessional wages | 70,321 | | |
| Support staff wages | 54,867 | | |
| Administrative salaries | 91,348 | | |
| Marketing salaries | 15,120 | | |
| **Subtotal - Salaries & Wages** | (1,012,580) | | |
| **Subtotal - Other Operating Expenses (Exh 6)** | (246,194) | | |
| **Total Operating Expenses** | | (1,258,774) | 83.89% |
| **NET INCOME FROM OPERATIONS** | | 127,868 | 8.52% |
| *Other Income & Expenses* | | | |
| Interest income | 2,423 | | |
| Interst expense | (16,517) | | |
| **Subtotal - Other Income & Expenses** | | (14,094) | 0.94% |
| **NET INCOME BEFORE TAXES** | | $113,774 | 7.58% |
| To arrive at net income after taxes, let's assume that Norton and West pay 30% of the net income before taxes of the business as personal income taxes. | | (34,132) | |
| Net Income After Taxes, or Margin | | $79,642 | 5.31% |

## Exhibit 6 - Other Expenses for the 2006 Income Statement

| *Other Operating Expenses* | |
|---|---:|
| Advertising | $3,575 |
| Bad debts | 21,048 |
| Computer repair & maintenance, supplies | 10,834 |
| Contributions | 8,804 |
| Copier | 4,832 |
| Depreciation | 38,490 |
| Dues, subscriptions, association expense | 2,699 |
| Insurance | 9,765 |
| Internet service | 2,639 |
| Janitorial services | 4,201 |
| Library, newsletters | 2,947 |
| Meals, entertainment, travel | 14,737 |
| Microfilm maintenance & supplies | 3,368 |
| Miscellaneous | 1,595 |
| Office supplies | 9,351 |
| Postage | 7,574 |
| Professional development | 24,698 |
| Professional services | 25,094 |
| Rent | 36,000 |
| Repair & maintenance - office | 1,768 |
| Telephone | 6,282 |
| Utilities | 5,893 |
| | |
| *Subtotal - Other Operating Expenses* | $246,194 |

| Exhibit 7 - Contribution Format Income Statement - Norton & West CPAs, L.L.C. | | | | | |
|---|---|---|---|---|---|
| | **2006** | | | **2007** | |
| Sales Revenue | $1,500,427 | 100.00% | | $1,531,048 | 100.00% |
| less Variable Expenses | (154,815) | 10.32% | | (157,374) | 10.28% |
| Contribution Margin | 1,345,612 | 89.68% | | 1,373,674 | 89.72% |
| less Fixed Expenses | (1,217,744) | 81.16% | | (1,234,485) | 80.63% |
| Net Income From Operations | $127,868 | 8.52% | | $139,189 | 9.09% |

**Exhibit 8 - December 31 Balance Sheet - Norton & West CPAs, L.L.C.**

| | 2006 | | 2007 |
|---|---|---|---|
| **ASSETS** | | | |
| *Current Assets* | | | |
| Cash | $98,617 | | $109,979 |
| Accounts Receivable | 150,682 | | 138,196 |
| Other Receivables | 1,548 | | 4,723 |
| Work in Process | 91,624 | | 77,630 |
| | | | |
| **Subtotal - Current Assets** | | $342,471 | $330,528 |
| | | | |
| *Fixed Assets* | | | |
| Computer Equipment | 84,692 | | 89,175 |
| Office Equipment | 41,811 | | 42,476 |
| Leasehold Improvements | 97,829 | | 97,829 |
| | | | |
| Total Cost | 224,332 | | 229,480 |
| Less - Accumulated Depreciation | (54,725) | | (89,832) |
| **Subtotal - Fixed Assets** | | 169,607 | 139,648 |
| | | | |
| *Intangible Assets* | | | |
| Goodwill | 14,328 | | 14,328 |
| | | | |
| **Subtotal - Intangible Assets** | | 14,328 | 14,328 |
| | | | |
| **TOTAL ASSETS** | | $526,406 | $484,504 |
| | | | |
| | | | |
| **LIABILITIES & OWNERS' EQUITY** | | | |
| *Current Liabilities* | | | |
| Accounts Payable | 15,396 | | 17,391 |
| Withheld Payroll Taxes | 39,285 | | 39,836 |
| Current Maturities - Notes | 48,793 | | 50,442 |
| | | | |
| **Subtotal - Current Liabilities** | | 103,474 | 107,669 |
| | | | |
| *Long-term Liabilities* | | | |
| Notes Payable -Net of Current Maturities | 202,804 | | 153,845 |
| | | | |
| **Subtotal - Long-term Liabilities** | | 202,804 | 153,845 |
| | | | |
| **TOTAL LIABILITIES** | | 306,278 | 261,514 |
| | | | |
| *Owners' Equity* | | | |
| Capital | 100,000 | | 100,000 |
| Retained Earnings | 120,128 | | 122,990 |
| | | | |
| **TOTAL OWNERS' EQUITY** | | 220,128 | 222,990 |
| | | | |
| **TOTAL LIABILITIES & OWNERS' EQUITY** | | $526,406 | $484,504 |
| | | | |
| | | | |
| **Average Total Assets Used During Year** | | $530,175 | $475,376 |

Please visit: www.howabusinessworks.com

CPSIA information can be obtained at www.ICGtesting.com
Printed in the USA
LVOW11s1619020914

402044LV00002B/585/P